YELLOW METAL

THE CROSS OF ST. STEPHEN

THE QUINTERO SAGA

by
PAUL W. LEBARON

Concho Flats Publishing

YELLOW METAL
THE CROSS OF ST. STEPHEN

International Standard Book Number 0-9717812-0-6
Copyright © by Paul W. LeBaron 1999

Events portrayed in this manuscript have no existence outside the imagination of the author and have no relation whatsoever to anyone bearing the same name or names. They are not even distantly inspired by an individual known or unknown to the author, and all incidents are pure invention by the author.

First printing, March 2002

ACKNOWLEDGEMENTS:

Cover art, Glen Stuart
Cover design, Dan Mills
Proofreading, Judy Caldwell and Kathy Brandenburg

Upon a crowded sheet,
My allotted time I pen.
One shares my dreams,
While writing her life with mine.

I dedicate this book to
My wife Jan

INTRODUCTION

YELLOW METAL
THE CROSS OF ST. STEPHEN

For hundreds of years, the Spanish, then the Mexicans, and finally, the Anglos, searched the Southwest for its treasure. Aztec gold created a lust unparalleled in history. Adventurers searched every point of the compass for the Yellow Metal in the New World.

Many mines were found and operated by the church; greed knew no bounds. Natives were baptized and introduced to chains, in that order. Rebellion often befell the priests, and death found them in some distant lonely place. So much wealth was at stake that the church and state quarreled over it. Finally the Robed Ones were called home and forbidden to return to New Spain.

To understand gold is to understand its nature. Being one of the heaviest substances on earth, as well as precious, made it hard to transport it to the king in Europe.

The remoteness of the Southwest lent the opportunity for gold to be found one day; only to be hidden the next to keep it "safe." Life, being fragile; many times the gold was never recovered and remains hidden to this day.

After the Gadsen Purchase, the lands south of the Gila River fell into the hands of the United States. The influx of people put the Apache Indians on edge; the Southwest was at war. The native people were trying to hold onto the lifestyle they followed from time beginning. The Whites wanted to subdue the earth and reap its harvest. Riches were out there to be found. Gold, silver, and copper mines were opened. Wealth was abundant to a lucky few, or unlucky as the case might be. Into this caldron rode men of all these cultures, all believing in their destiny, which required them to forge a relationship based on need; a need for God, gold and glory. These needs so finely interwoven at times were almost one, yet, at other times come unwove to strangle the unsuspecting.

This is a fictional account of how the interaction between the Indians, Mexicans and Anglos might have been. Very few records were kept by the players; so much room is left for speculation.

THE QUINTERO SAGA CONTINUES.....

CONTENTS

PREVIEW
CRY OF THE EAGLE
THE CRYING BABY
CHAPTER 1

YELLOW METAL
THE QUINTERO SAGA
PROLOGUE

Quintero had been to this place many times, the fort below Mt. Graham. It was here, as a young warrior, he had waited three days to see if any more white eyes returned for yellow metal. This was before the soldiers came and built here. His father and four other braves overtook two such men in search of this metal the white men crave so much. They were quickly killed and their belongings and bodies put in the hole they had dug. Then all the ore they had been saving was carefully returned to Mother Earth. All sign of mining was erased. Quintero had been positioned to watch and see if anyone else knew of this mine. High in the rocks above, he could see for a day's journey to the south, and a half day's journey to the east and west. The sacred mountain rose high to his back. This was Quintero's first important assignment as a young man. He would soon be a warrior and fight along side of his father and kin; yes, he would always remember this place which was called "Metate Mound." For here lay evidence that his people had been here forever. Stone bowls littered the area where generations had come to grind acorns in season and put on fat to sustain them through the lean months of winter.

Because water was plentiful, the Longknives put their fort here. He did not enjoy doing business with these soldiers, but fighting had long since been put aside. Cochise had died. Geronimo had surrendered and been taken away. This much he knew; the once great warrior would never set foot on this sacred spot again. It was left to the old men like him to remember how it was. A lot had happened since those three days in his youth. Quintero thought it funny now, as he stood on the commissary porch and looked to the north. Not a sign of the workings of the richest rocks of yellow metal he had ever seen was there for the eyes to see. He and the others had done their job well. All the many, many Longknives who lived now within a stone's throw of this place would never find it. Soon the secret would die with him.

This place and many hands' worth of fingers in number were hidden in much the same way. It had stopped the advancement of the white man to this area for many years; of this, he was proud.

Quintero now lived to the north on a reservation that had been assigned to his people. He had escaped being taken with Geronimo, by marrying a woman of his cousins' clan from the banks of the Salt River. He had remained with her people when Geronimo broke away the last time and fled to Mexico.

He was forever grateful for this because, even after the fighting had stopped, he was able to hide the old mines that dotted the land.

The Spaniards, then the Mexicans and finally, the Whites had searched for such places. It had been shown to him in a dream that this was his cause here on Mother Earth. The Great Spirit gave him the strength to wander these mountains for a lifetime to do this.

Quintero often hung around the settlements of the white men to learn the comings and goings of the prospectors, or "burro men," working the area. Much could be learned with one's eyes and ears. Quintero was able to follow the tracks of the best of them. The "burro men" had grown very clever in hiding their tracks, in circling back to see if they were being followed. To his reckoning, he had never betrayed his presence to any of them until he wanted to. By working alone, he was able to suprise many of them in the act of digging yellow metal. Up close, he could look in their eyes as he plunged a knife in their belly. He preferred this method of punishment, because as they died, they knew they had done wrong. For this land was sacred and belonged to his people. Mother Earth and her twin, the Sky, were one, and his people revered them both.

Not all were killed; however, some that gave up easily and would leave were treated differently. Sometimes a good scare would do. Other times they might be chased for many days before becoming disoriented, seldom finding the way back to their diggings.

Everyone has heard of the famous Lost Dutchman Mine. A vein of gold, wider than a man's hand, formed by a violent thrust from the bowels of the earth. A vein so rich, that a man could live a lifetime by breaking off a few pieces; or die trying. The Dutchman knew better than to return; an arrow waited him if he tried.

Quintero had a hand in keeping the Adams' diggings from being relocated. His father and a group of warriors intercepted the Adams' party as they passed the foot of the sacred mountain. They followed the party for many days. Eventually they caught up with them and killed most of the miners. Adams escaped and spent the rest of his life trying to find the mine again, but to no avail. Quintero and others guarded it and kept its whereabouts secret. As the floods uncovered this vast deposit of nuggets, new soil had to be brought in to replace the old, so as to keep it hidden. To this day it remains so.

The Saunder's Mine was the same. That rich ore had to be mined by Quintero and taken to a nearby cave to be hidden as it was so visible. The remaining ledge was altered to hide any sign of being changed.

Thus, a lifetime had been spent in this cause. None except a few family members knew of Quintero's quest, and some chiefs and members of his clan were also called upon at times to help out. He had been successful; to date, most of the mines in Apacheria had been sealed. The trafficking in gold in other areas was also stopped, for awhile, from passing through to Mexico. Skeleton Canyon had become littered with the bones of the dead caravan packers. This gold was also hidden so as not to be found again.

When Quintero's father died, he promised him his cause would not die as long as he, Quintero, had a breath of life within him. So it was from that day on that Quintero, like his father, was responsible to the Great Spirit to seek out, find and bury all the mines he could.

Quintero had heard the stories many times of how the men with hair on their face had come across the great waters. They brought horses to ride; they had skin of steel, which no arrow could pierce. They also had guns that sounded as thunder. With the horses and arms, they made war with the great clans to the south, which brought total ruin to them. The Aztecs fell under their wrath. Their great Chief Montezuma was executed, and his kingdom was divided among the conquering armies. Most of his vast wealth fell into Spanish hands.

Just as a rock is thrown into the water and rings, one after another, grows bigger and reaches further and further away, such were the Spanish. They came like these ever-reaching rings, further and further, searching the earth for gold. Clans that cooperated and helped them find yellow metal was put into slavery, mining and hauling to New Spain.

Word began to travel just like the ever-reaching rings as well. Quintero's father's people were warned to hide all signs and traces of the yellow metal. As word spread from one to another, some areas were saved. At least some time was bought so that they could live undisturbed a few more years. Thanks to Quintero and others like him, this had been accomplished.

THE CROSS OF ST. STEPHEN
Chapter 1

Father Antonne was born in Seville, Spain. He was an orphan, so no one knew the exact date of his birth, but it was at the height of the Spanish exploration of the New World. It was an exciting time and he wanted to be part of it. In due time he would teach Christ to the heathen and his whole life was dedicated to this purpose. Educated in a church school and trained in the way of the cloth, he had heard all the stories coming out of New Spain since his youth, of how wealth was found on these new continents for the taking—as well as souls enough to lay in store for eternity. He would do his best to follow in the footsteps of those who had walked before him. Coronado had explored the vast lands to the north. It had been his intention since becoming a priest, to go to these northern provinces and teach these natives.

Father Antonne was delayed a few years as he was sent first to St. Augustine, a thriving port on the Atlantic. He made the best of it; being a positive man by nature, knowing that in due time, he would be called upon to serve in the far away lands that Coronado brought under the flag of the King of Spain.

The King's nephew was the Viceroy of all the frontier lands of New Spain. It was he who had the great cross of gold put together by the best artisans of Mexico City. Aztec gold was melted down and reworked into a massive crucifix with ten of the biggest emeralds left in the provinces. Inside a small tubular opening were two bones of a Saint, believed to be St. Stephen's. All this was intended to bring good fortune to the settling and building of a string of missions among the Pueblos, starting at Cibola. If all went well, this would be the first of many. Father Antonne had long before designed a plan that would eventually extend missions throughout the northern lands of New Mexico, and beyond.

Things went well for a few years, but eventually the stern discipline of the Robed Ones made the people, who were used to a life much different than theirs, conspire to throw off the yoke placed upon them.

The Pueblo Indians mounted a revolt that took the lives of most of the Priests residing in the Southwest. Father Antonne befriended an Indian man who had long been a servant at his Mission. The man did not expose all the plan of the uprising, but Father Antonne put together enough pieces to know danger was at hand. He took the Cross of St. Stephen to a secret hiding place where it temporarily would be safe. He also hid the important records for the Mission.

The next few days, he was alert to the many changes in the behavior of the villagers.

Father Antonne, being one to trust in God, but then use all the resources on hand, began to stockpile enough food and provisions to mount a retreat to safety.

The hour came when he knew he must go, or forever leave his bones scattered upon the plains. His bones were nothing special, but the Cross of St. Stephen must be protected by the lives of the Saints.

Father Antonne left in the night; two teamsters accompanied him. They took an ox cart and four pack animals with them. They were carrying the Cross of St. Stephen, water, food and weapons.

Daylight found them many miles from Cibola. The ground was frozen and they left no tracks so the wolves (scouts) following them remained unsuccessful. Father Antonne knew time was of the essence, so sleep was rationed. One man rested in the back of the cart, the other two kept the animals and equipment moving.

A fierce storm was brewing to the north. Father Antonne decided, after the second day, they had better make a decent camp with shelter sufficient to withstand the coming bitterness. The animals were hobbled short, in case the storm raged for several days. Father Antonne committed their fate to the hands of God, and a deep sleep fell upon them.

The third day, the sky cleared, but no warmth was to be found. A steady wind continued to blow from the north. It took a half day to find the livestock. They had let the snow pile high over them to hold the heat against their bodies. Father Antonne kept a watchful eye on the horizons and a prayer in his heart. He knew they were being followed. He also knew that the same storm stopping them fell equally as hard on his pursuers. Still, no time could be wasted. Safety lay ahead, if only it could be reached in time. They continued to make their way along the Zuni River. Tusayan lay ahead; surely the peaceful Hopis would offer them refuge.

As they approached Stinky Springs, a Hopi Indian, who had accepted the Sign of the Cross, intercepted them. He told of how the Robed Ones in the Hopitah Villages had been thrown over the cliffs. The village, which had accepted the message the Robed Ones had been destroyed, their men killed and the women and children divided among the remaining villages. He fled for his life to warn others to beware. Father Antonne assured the Indian that the same fate had befallen all in the villages of Cibola.

Father Antonne invited the Hopi to join him in a flight for safety. Under the circumstances, he readily agreed. He was armed and was put in the front to ride point.

They tried to head east at Stinky Springs, but was turned back by those who were following them. Next, they turned southwest trying to avoid a confrontation. They held this course as much as possible. This way they skirted the timberline extending into the great badlands of the Navajo. This was no man's land and, by taking this course, Father Antonne hoped to pass unencountered by hostile Indians. When they reached the Little Colorado River, they stayed to the north bank and followed along it. Upon reaching the fork of fresh water flowing from the south, they camped for two days. Rest was badly needed for man and beast.

Father Antonne and others were out hunting for some camp meat when they saw horsemen on the horizon to the north. Many men were on the move and headed towards their camp. The Navajos were still a great distance away, but the large party of men and animals were clearly visible upon the snow.

"Damn," Father Antonne said to himself. The fresh water lay directly by their camp. "Even a fool should have known better!" he said loudly. The only hope was in out running the Navajos to camp, gathering up their things and fleeing.

Father Antonne yelled loudly, "Run for your lives, as well as for the safety of the Cross of St. Stephen; for the Saints. Run!"

A good mile lay between them and their camp. They were on foot except for a pack animal. Father Antonne cast off his great robe and mounted the animal. He rode off in haste, one hand rested against the two pistols in his belt. Onward he drove his animal. He knew he must warn his fellows in camp of the impending danger. Also, an escape must be made, for the safety of the Cross of St. Stephen lay at stake.

Father Antonne arrived at the camp just as the Navajos' drew nigh. He was able to help silence the animals. They held their hands over the animals' noses so they could not alert the incoming band of their presence. Father Antonne, from his hiding place in the willows, watched the Navajos approach. He knew it would only be a matter of time until they were discovered. He signaled to the others to retreat, as he led the way. Cover was sparse, so they had to head up the stream. A dangerous game ensued, with them sneaking away, while the Navajos quickly spread out and established a perimeter. Dogs were barking loudly and splashing in the water as the red men rode along the creek. A few minutes of opportunity were all they could hope for.

Father Antonne, ever the one to appreciate small favors, rapidly retreated to the south. He quickly turned the animals toward the cliffs above the stream. They stayed high where they could keep an eye on their backs. The ox cart caught up with them sometime in the night. It had been hidden a short distance from the Navajos and waited for darkness before it continued.

Father Antonne knew it was no longer possible to think of reaching safety to the north. He feared the Rio Grande settlements suffered the same fate. So safety could only be reached to the south. The stream came from that direction and they eagerly followed it, for it led away from the Navajos. The next morning, they were once again camped by the stream. The water ran clear and fast. The four men were still resting when the first sound of hoofs pounded the earth.

"Up, up!" yelled Father Antonne. "The Devil be upon us."

His three teamsters were up in a second; the animals were hastily retrieved and flight was underway. They turned due east as cover was to be found along a dry waterway. They used this to their advantage, and once again, avoided the wrath of the Navajos. Three miles from the waterway, they reached the treeless plains; they tried to head south, but to no avail. The Navajo trackers stood in their way.

They carefully headed east until they bogged down in the mud. Thinking if they could make it until night, the ground would freeze enough to let them cross. This is where darkness found them. During the night they tried to get the cart and animals through the mud, but it was bottomless, and it did not freeze enough to support their weight. The pack animals and ox fought hard to make it through the partly frozen ground. Father Antonne had tied them all to the cart trying to pull it out of the mire. The tethers broke, and in the confusion, the animals bolted and ran off in the night. The teamsters were in pursuit, but the animals turned and headed towards the camp of the Navajos. The men returned to Father Antonne empty-handed. The ox alone remained, and they decided to kill and eat it, as it would soon fall into the hands of the enemy. Hunger had stalked them since they left Cibola; now they would eat well. The cart was not much, but it was the only fortification they possessed. They turned it on its side and waited for morning, hiding as best they could behind it.

The horsemen came at daylight. Two teamsters fell on the first wave; they were lanced to death shortly after discharging their muskets. One Navajo horse fell dead receiving a ball to its chest. The Indians fought on undeterred. Father Antonne seized the only opportunity that presented itself. He grabbed the great knife he carried at his side. With two blows, the heads of the teamsters were severed from their bodies. He quickly hung the Cross of St. Stephen, which was enclosed in its iron case, in a nearby cedar tree. The heads of the two teamsters were then tied, one on each side of the cross. Lastly, he stood tall with his blood-covered hands in the air reaching towards the Heavens.

"This thing I do for the Cross of St. Stephen!" he said loudly.

He turned and ran towards the Navajos. They thought he was truly a demon from another world. Dead men were not to be touched and they no longer had any interest in the tree with the heads hanging in it, nor of this mad Spaniard.

The Hopi looked on in horror. Father Antonne single handily backed off a whole band of his enemies. He had expected sure death at their hands. Now, perhaps, death lay at the hands of this mad man. Yet, he had no other to turn to in this land of his enemy.

Father Antonne came walking back. He collapsed onto the ground, drained of strength.

When he finally spoke, he said to the remaining man, "Let's burn the ox cart so they will get no use from it, then flee before the enemy can fall upon us again."

Father Antonne looked back at the cedar tree containing the cross and the heads of his former friends. Smoke billowed into the sky from the burning cart. Darkness would soon fall, and many miles must be put between them and the Navajos this night.

God alone could protect the cross from here on. With a quick prayer, Father Antonne turned to the south and broke into a slow run, the Hopi right at his heels.

VINCENT MILES
Chapter 2

Vincent Miles had ridden hard, trying to put as much distance as a man could on horseback in a day. He had left Prescott in a hurry. He couldn't believe how big a chump he could be. All the money in the world lay at his feet for the taking. Yet he passed it up for twenty-five years or better. He always camped by an old iron cross put there by some Spaniard, who knows when? By doing so, he unwillingly, had become a part of all this. Had he not found the bones of some Christian on the plains two days north of the cross? Yet he, being a sentimental fool, packed a tarp full of bones of this pilgrim many miles to the Spanish cross. He added them to the bones of many placed there by unknown travelers. Thus, this place became a shrine, because of the cross, the iron cross, the sign of the cross, in a land of disbelief. Therefore, like the rest, he placed bones of the unfortunate around this iron cross so they could, at least, find rest in a strange land claimed by a red man who had no use for the Whites.

Now, a turn of events had drawn Vincent Miles out of retirement. He had hunted antelope on a plain adjoining a tributary of the Little Colorado, where, at his favorite camp he could always count on getting an antelope and grilling it to perfection. He thought back to the day he discovered the rusty cross. It was a day when he thought he would surely die of starvation, a day when the beaver trapping had been so poor that a man forgot about catching fur; he just wanted a carcass to eat upon. Beaver meat is very good, but his traps were empty. That day he jumped an antelope buck and chased it all the way to the bog east of the expanse of plains beyond Silver Creek, east of where it enters the rock cliffs before heading to the Little Colorado. He did not find the iron cross per se; it found him. He actually was vain enough to think he was the first white man to set foot on this place. His antelope was cooking on a fire of cedar coals. He could smell it fifty yards from camp as he walked to find adequate feed for his two horses. After hobbling them, while returning to camp, under a cedar tree almost hidden in the shade, he saw a cross, rusty in color. He got on his hands and knees and crawled under the branch of the tree for a closer look. The writing was in strange verse; he could not recollect ever seeing it before. He figured that some Spaniard had died there. And, luckily for him, he had a friend to erect a cross over his grave. Vincent paid it no thought, that perhaps it meant more than this. He accepted life as it was presented to him. A cross was a cross, a sign of deep belief in something. While on his knees, he offered a quick prayer in behalf of himself, as well as the fallen Spaniard. He asked questions, but just did not see anymore in it than this.

Now he found himself headed up the Verde trail; the Mogollon Rim lay ahead. He would ride one horse and lead the other one, so it could catch its air. He would ride day and night, if necessary. Many years, yes, a lifetime of sleeping with one eye open, would enable him to reach his old antelope camp before the Mexican.

The Mexican showed up in Prescott several days before. Vincent couldn't believe his fortune. He had been having a drink by Fort Whipple, when in walked a sight for sore eyes. He thought, at first, he was an Indian who had been back east. This poor fella had clothing on that would make him noticed, no matter where he was. A Mexican dandy no doubt, he walked up to Vincent and asked if he could have a seat. Vincent replied he didn't own the place to sit down. The Mexican then began to drink, drink heavily, as if to wash down all the dust between there and Mexico City. Vincent kept a beer to his mouth, as well. Luckily for him he didn't take it out much. Because this night was different than the rest of his life, this night lady luck had finally smiled. He knew it was a night for listening. The Mexican had been on a mission for several weeks in an attempt to return honor to his family's name, but the road had been all up hill from Mexico. He had worked for years to obtain permission from his country and church to search for the missing cross. Now he faced a turn of events he had not foreseen, a second government to deal with. That is what he came to Prescott for, to visit with the new territorial government, and obtain permission to search the eastern part of the territory for a certain artifact lost by the Catholic Church. It was after much drinking; the Mexican confided in Vincent about the "Cross of St. Stephen" lost by his great, great grandfather in the vast expanse of land west of Cibola. Vincent was just a plain man, unschooled in the value of great wealth. But, even he knew this was an opportunity unheard of in his lifetime. He bid the Mexican good night and headed back to his quarters on the edge of town.

His had been a lonely life for a number of years. His Indian wife had returned to her people when he had quit trapping and moved to the new city of Prescott. "Just as well," he thought; "he didn't need her anymore, anyway." Truth is, she had kept the Indians from killing him for many years as he worked the streams of the Northern Arizona territory. Still, he missed her on the lonely nights. "She was a good person to have around," he thought, as he pushed his horse onward. "If this works out I'll look her up."

After climbing the rim, he crowded his horses' onward turning northeasterly towards the Little Colorado. He skirted the timberlands until reaching the cliffs of Clear Creek, then north to the Chevlon Bad Lands. He rested by Horsehead Crossing, then turned south towards Silver Creek. He rode on, pushing his animals to their limits. Upon reaching his destination, he found that several families of Mormons had taken possession of the lands he thought only good for trapping. They were busily engaged in trying to get a crop in the ground. Women, as well as their men, were tilling the soil. Vincent rested his horses for a moment and wiped the dirt from his forehead with a bandana. He then rode towards the east before the Mormons had time to ask him any questions. He only hoped they had not ventured eastward to the antelope flats, and by chance, discovered the cross that the Mexican called the "Cross of St. Stephen."

Halfway to the place where the cross stood, Vincent passed several Mormon young-uns herding a small band of milk cows and a few head of horses. From that point on, hoof prints littered the ground continuously. Vincent began to feel doubt that the cross could remain undiscovered by so many people. He rode his horse up a slight knoll he had been to many times. This is where he always camped. Fifty yards below on the other side stood the cross. Could this be the one he searched for? Vincent jumped off his horses and tied them to a nearby cedar. Walking quickly to the cross, he dropped to his knees and crawled under the over hanging branches. He paused for a moment, then noticed the cross had sunk into the ground more than on previous visits. The arms of the cross were barely visible. He moved closer and ran his hands over its surface. The iron had grown rough to the touch. He pushed against the cross. It would not move. He braced himself and shook it more vigorously; still no movement. He stood up and went to his horse and retrieved a small spade. He carefully dug around the cross and then proceeded to move it slightly. Soon it was loose from the earth. Vincent raised it carefully. Part of the iron cover had rusted away below the ground. The gold cross alone extended into the earth. Vincent fell over backward pulling the cross to him. He rolled over and released the upper part of the cross from its former prison. The sun caught sight of the cross for the first time in one hundred and eighty years. Its beauty held Vincent spellbound. The emeralds were like looking in the eyes of a beautiful woman. They made him feel warm on the inside. For hours he rotated the cross and examined it from all the angles possible. It was much larger than he imagined it would be. The workmanship was exquisite, the likes of which Vincent had not dreamed of.

Darkness was soon upon him. He came to his senses and realized he had lost track of the time. The golden cross would have to be put aside and matters at hand attended to.

After a meal of hard tack, Vincent put his bedroll under the cedar tree that the cross had stood under all this time.

"This night, then this cross and I will be on our way," Vincent thought.

Vincent tossed restlessly all night. Morning came early. Too many plans had to be worked out to waste time in sleep. A lifetime had to be lived in the days left for him. His previous time had only been a life of toil. Now a life of comfort and luxury lay ahead. The cross would allow him that. Out of respect, he returned the iron case to its former position. At least the dead would have a marker over them. It's all that showed before. Most of the bones had long since decayed. Vincent carefully wrapped the gold cross in a blanket and then put it on the tarpaulin he always carried around his bedroll. Several cedar sticks were cut to make a brace around the cross to alter its shape. It now looked like a crude pack frame that was on the horse being led. Vincent would tell any askers he was going to purchase supplies. No one would be the wiser. He then took the gold cross a half-mile further east and dug a hole big enough to accommodate the cross in its new bundle. It would not be safe to take it where he was going. He would do what he had to do, return for the cross, and then be on his way back to Prescott.

Vincent headed south up Silver Creek amazed at the amount of land the Mormons were putting under cultivation.

He could not remember for sure how many years it had been since he was last here, but time never stood still. He, on the other hand, had grown quite sedentary in his behavior. This would change. A fork in the trail came quickly, and once again he was climbing into the timber. A feeling of freshness, rebirth, he couldn't put a handle on it, filled his being. It must be the excitement of finding the golden cross. He would make an effort to locate his woman and try to get her to come with him to Prescott. Then after getting his affairs in order, they would go on to San Francisco. There a proper sum could be attained for the golden cross.

Many thoughts filled Vincent's mind as he headed toward the village where his wife was from. Show Low Creek lay below him. He planned on following it to the Mogollon Rim. Beyond it was the Indian Agency at Ft. Apache.

HECTOR ANTONNE
Chapter 3

Hector Antonne figured he had wasted a good week trying to gain audience with the new territorial Governor of Arizona. When he finally was summoned to his office, permission was forthcoming without any trouble. The Governor was sympathetic to his family's quest to try to find the "Cross of St. Stephen," and once again return honor to his family name. The Governor listened inquisitively as Hector laid out a tale that happened almost two centuries ago. He told it as if it happened just yesterday, a tale of a young Priest, sent to the New World to preach to the Indians at Cibola. The priest was given a very valuable artifact, commissioned in celebration of this great event. It was hoped that eventually these missions would cover much of the Southwest. Instead, Father Antonne barely escaped the revolts of the Indians with his life. He abandoned the great "Cross of St. Stephen" somewhere in northeastern Arizona. Father Antonne almost starved to death before he reached the village of Tubac where the military had recently established an outpost. He eventually worked his way back to Mexico City. There he was excommunicated from the Catholic Church and his priesthood nullified. He was devastated to learn he was also banished from his homeland by the King of Spain. Father Antonne eventually married a native woman, and hence began the Antonne family tree in the Americas.

Father Antonne sought backing most of his life to gather a party of men to mount an effort to retrieve the great cross and clear his name. But without the church's blessing, he was unsuccessful. The church confiscated his diaries and maps of his journeys in the lands of Cibola and Tusayan. Finally, after much perseverance, they were once again put in the family's hands. "Some say it was by many pesos that his Uncle was able to open doors heretofore left closed. It is for his interest I am here. He took me in and raised me as a son," Hector Antonne continued, "I, like Grandpa Antonne, was an orphan, and it might be my purpose to restore his honor since we are kindred spirits. He was Hector Antonne of old; I am Hector Antonne, the new. Sir, I am here to restore the aforementioned honor once held dear to my family, now lost for a long time, many lifetimes, I am sad to report."

The Governor rose to his feet and walked towards Hector with an outstretched arm. "Permission is granted, sir. Go with my country's blessing."

Hector thanked the Governor, shook his hand and went to the outer office to retrieve a letter the Governor had written for him as an introduction to "Whom it may concern."

Hector's first stop would be an army fort in central Arizona, closest to the area where the cross was lost. It would be his intention to secure a guide who was familiar with the area. He would also try to examine the maps of the military and compare them to the maps and diaries of Father Antonne. Perhaps, something would match between them. A needle was waiting out there somewhere in a giant haystack. Hector needed a miracle, he knew, but he couldn't help but feel positive. After all, he would soon be walking in the footsteps of Father Antonne.

He secured provisions and was soon upon his way. He traveled the Verde Trail up over the rim and on to Ft. Apache, located on the White River. He found the military very helpful and willing to share what information they had. A few landmarks possibly matched, but it would be necessary to do field work to verify them.

Hector was busily engaged in trying to enlist the help of a scout and guide when Vincent Miles came riding down the middle of the road. Their eyes met for a moment. A puzzled look appeared on Hector's face, one that met a sullen stare from Vincent. The surprise only showed for a moment. Then smiles appeared on both faces

"Señor!" Hector Antonne said loudly. "I am surprised to see you once again."

"Yes," replied Vincent Miles. "I was unaware your destination was here."

Hector continued, "Yes, I am currently seeking to employ a guide for my expedition. Is it merely coincidence of our meeting, or is there more to this than what meets the eye?"

Vincent asked dryly, "What do you mean?"

"I just know this is a big world, señor, and after our conversation the other night over drinks, I am wondering if you might perhaps have motives of your own."

"I assure you, Señor Hector, it is but a chance meeting here. I have come to seek out my former missus. She left me sometime back and I want to talk to her about starting something fresh. That is all. I might be of some use to you though. I know this area about as well as anyone."

"Indeed, sir. You did not tell me that at our last meeting."

"It is not always wise to tell all you know in this wild country, Mister." With that, he spurred his mount onward.

"Not so fast, Señor Miles. Perhaps it is more than chance our meeting again. Get down and let's talk!"

Hector Antonne grew uneasy sitting around Ft. Apache. He began to wonder if he did the right thing hiring Vincent Miles to be his guide and scout. He worried he had confided in him too much information about the Cross of St. Stephen. The fewer who knew the value of what they were looking for the better. Now, not only did Vincent know too much about the lost artifact, he also knew the country better than anyone he had met so far did. Yes, a sick feeling began to fill his craw. "Perhaps Señor Vincent holds all the aces currently," thought Hector Antonne.

Hector spent his time pouring over the military maps of the area where he planned to search. He compared his great, great grandfather's maps and diaries to the more up-to-date maps, and found a few landmarks that might match. One big round mesa seemed to be on all the maps. The Little Colorado and the Silver Creek drainage was also a match. So it seemed that the area was narrowed down somewhat. One hundred and eighty years is a long time. He hoped that from the landmarks he could find the location where his great, great grandfather had abandoned the cross.

He could not afford to let doubt enter his mind, so he shifted his thoughts to his horses. He walked briskly to where he had them stabled. Upon entering a dark alley, a large Indian man approached him.

"I hear you are wanting a party of men to search for gold?"

"Who asks this question of me?" Hector Antonne inquired. "Step out into the light and let's talk."

"No," replied the Indian. "A man hears a lot around the forts of the long knives. I give you warning that Indian gold stays here. Return to your home and live!" The Indian turned to leave.

Hector protested, "Señor, please allow me another moment of your time."

With that the Indian halted and turned once again to face the Mexican.

"I do not search for just any gold. I search for something lost long ago by my ancestor. He brought it with him from Mexico. It was abandoned here because of an attack by hostile men. I only seek that to which I am entitled. I do not wish to mine or defraud anyone out of anything. My great, great grandfather was a Catholic Priest on a mission to you Indian people. When he lost the artifact entrusted to him, he lost face and his honor. He was removed from his holy office and died in shame. I only seek to restore his honor by returning what was lost back to its original owners. That is all, sir. I assure you."

"Tell me more about this man," asked the Indian.

"His name was Father Hector Antonne. He was sent to the land of Cibola, now called Zuni. He followed in the footsteps of the General Coronado. During a revolt, he took a certain artifact and tried to escape to safety. Instead, he was overpowered somewhere north of here. He, and one Indian man, escaped death and returned to Mexico and, instead of being welcomed as returning heroes, my great, great grandfather was ruined."

"Yes," the Indian said, "I have heard stories of this escape. The Navajos called him the Sly One. It is handed down by the old ones that he escaped the Zuni, then the Navajo, and he made his way through Apacheria as well. He hung the heads of the two men by an iron cross. This became a land of the dead to the Navajos. They would not go close to the cross again. The

Whites brought the bones of the fallen believers in the white God here. It became a shrine. As far as I know, it still remains so. It is this iron cross that you seek," the big Indian asked, 'or is there more?"

Hector did not know how to answer the question. He had already told Vincent Miles too much. Now, he risked doing it again to an Indian whose face he could not even see.

"Come. Walk with me," Hector invited. Together, they proceeded to the stable. "What is your name?" Hector asked.

"Quintero," the Indian replied.

Once inside, Hector could see he was talking to a man far above the average size. He could see a whisper of gray forming in his hair. Something about this man demanded respect. He could also sense a genuine concern. He did not know why. To date, most of the red men only ignored him.

"Meet me here in the morning and we will talk some more," Hector replied.

Without a word, Quintero, once again, became part of the darkness.

Hector returned to his room and took out his great, great grandfather's papers. He studied them late into the night.

THE APACHE WOMAN
Chapter 4

Hector was a man who was open. You could tell he was honest. It showed on his face, yet he had mystery in his eyes. It was almost, as if he looked through you at times. Vincent wondered if Hector was looking into him at this moment and, if so, what was he seeing? A strange turn of events had just happened. Vincent Miles had always been capable of doing what was necessary to get a job done. At this time he not only had the "Cross of St. Stephen" hidden where only he knew its whereabouts, but now he was in the employ of the man who had tipped him off to its existence in the first place. Even though the cross was worth fabulous wealth, he had no other immediate prospect for keeping beans on his plate. So, work he must, even if it were for this dandy from Mexico. Señor Antonne had given him a small advance to buy what supplies he needed. He would sleep in a real bed tonight, take a bath, eat a steak for dinner, and then look up a certain Apache woman he had not seen for awhile. He leisurely spent the afternoon preparing himself as planned. He also pulled a bottle from his bedroll and took a deep swallow.

He rode up East Fork for a few miles, then stopped, and took several more swigs from the bottle. It put him a jovial mood. Upon reaching the rancheria, he jumped off his horse and began to tie him to a low branch of a tree close to a brush wiki-up. A dog barked at his heels as he walked closer. A flap went up and several Indians appeared from within. None of them looked familiar to him. Finally, an old man made his way out of the interior of the dwelling.

"Who is it you seek?" he asked.

"The runaway woman who lived with the trapper up on the rim, and had two children by him," Vincent replied.

"Are you that man?" the old one asked.

"Yes, I am," Vincent said. "She has left us for the home of Quintero. His wife is her sister."

Vincent knew his audience with the red men was over. They turned their backs to him and returned to their hut. He remounted his horse and rode back to Fort Apache.

He would have to work fast. Hector would be expecting to ride out with him in two days. Vincent had needed that much time to settle some business with his former companion. Daybreak found him in the saddle riding a rough trail of rim rock, looking down upon the White River. After several miles, he reached the union with the Black River. At this point it became the Salt. Beyond, the canyon widened into a small valley. It was here he was told, he would find the Quintero family ranch. He could smell cedar smoke before he could actually see their lodging. Dogs sounded the general alarm and children began appearing around him as he drew close to the cluster of dwellings. From the corner of his eye, he saw a giant of a man coming towards him. Resting his hand on a large bladed knife at his side.

"I am here to see a woman; one I've not seen for sometime. She is the mother of my children. I hear she is with you. Is this the Quintero Rancheria?" Vincent asked.

"Yes, I am Quintero."

"I am Vincent Miles. I wish to speak with the woman Roberta."

As if by magic, Roberta appeared as he spoke her name. She seemed reasonably happy to see him. After all, it had been several years. He did not know what type of reception he would receive. They walked down by the river and talked. Consumption had claimed the lives of their children. Some say it was from living too close to the soldiers at Ft. Apache that gave the youngsters the disease. She had returned to his camp once by Silver Creek on a fall hunting trip. They had been successful in killing some antelope, and making jerky of them, but she could see his camp had been unused. She was at the house of her sister, intending to also become Quintero's wife. It had not happened yet, and it made her heart glad that he had returned.

Vincent was saddened by the news that his children were dead, more for Roberta than himself, though. He had left them and started a new life. Had he not? Yes, it was so. Therefore, it was she who was there caring for them and watching them die that had the hardest lot. Somehow, knowing how she must have suffered made him want to make it up to her.

"Come with me now, Roberta!" he pleaded.

"First we must seek the permission of Quintero," she replied. "He has been my guardian and provider."

They returned to Quintero's home. He was outside roasting a piece of meat on a stick as they walked up.

"I wish to go with this man, my former husband," Roberta said.

Quintero did not look up. He continued to gaze into the fire.

"Does my sister's husband see good in our future?" asked Roberta.

"What are your plans with this woman?" Quintero asked Vincent.

"I will take her to wife and care for her as my own," Vincent's replied.

"What will you do?" Quintero asked.

"I am going to be in the hire of a Mexican in search of an artifact of gold long ago lost by a Padre who was living at the Zuni Pueblo, a village far from here," answered Vincent.

Quintero still did not look up, nor did he change his expression. At the mention of gold, old thoughts and resentments began to stir in his mind. He did not have the power to stop this woman from leaving with this man; it was only out of respect she had asked him. But new reservations entered Quintero's mind. Perhaps, one day they would meet again on unfriendly terms. "Go then!" was all he said as he got up and walked over to his shelter.

Vincent waited for her to pack her few belongings. He could sense that this giant Indian named Quintero was sizing him up. He was glad Roberta's sister was married to him. Perhaps this mattered, maybe not. He could sense something changed when he mentioned the word gold. Then, perhaps, he was figuring too hard, he thought.

They rode back toward Fort Apache in the dark for awhile. Finally they stopped to make a bed in a grove of cedars overlooking the river below. As the water jumped from one rapid to another, Vincent and Roberta worked out the tension that had been built up over the years of absence from each other.

Vincent knew he had done wrong by leaving this woman so long ago. The attention she had just given him made him feel alive, more so than he had for sometime. Yes, he was right, he thought to himself as he walked down to check on his horses. This woman is something special. She has the ability to anchor him to a world so foreign, to the white roots he came from, in a land that could give, yet take so quickly.

Vincent Miles had an appointment to keep with his new employer. But there on the White River, in the arms of an Apache woman, he found it hard to press on and keep his schedule. He, and the woman, was splashing in the water when Quintero overtook them. Unnoticed, he continued on to the Military Post.

For one of the few times in his life, Vincent was content. He had forgotten how much he loved this bronze woman. She had endured a lot with him in his trapping days. Yes, they had been happy, but not content. You become content knowing you control your destiny. For once he felt as if this were so, thanks to the golden cross-hidden back at his antelope hunting camp. Perhaps, he should just hook up with the cross and leave the Mexican high and dry. It would probably be the most humane thing to do, thought Vincent. Hector would never see the cross anyway, at least not the gold one. He would have to be content with returning to Mexico with the empty iron cross, the iron case that once kept the giant gold crucifix protected. Vincent closed his eyes for a moment, and once again could see the emeralds glistening. The woman approached him from behind and rested her hand on his back. He jumped, realizing that having a woman around would take a little getting used to again.

Vincent decided he must return to Ft. Apache and honor his commitment to the Mexican, Hector Antonne. To not do so, would draw suspicion to him. If he led the Mexican dandy to where he could find the iron cross, it would look as if the Crucifix was taken by someone else. After all, it was out there in the muddy flats for almost two centuries. He would then have fulfilled all he intended on doing. At a given moment, when the timing was right, he could make his way back to Prescott and then on to San Francisco with the golden cross. These thoughts once again seemed right to Vincent Miles. After all, he was a simple man, a man, who at one time considered this vast expanse of Arizona home. For most of his life, he was the only white man to do so. Then, one by one, they came, prospectors, ranchers and then the military. Then the hay gatherers who supplied hay for them followed. The meat hunters were next, now the Mormons.

Throughout all the years the cross remained in its place, as Father Antonne had left it. Vincent wondered how many other people actually knew of its location. Other bones had been placed around the cross, besides the ones he had put there. This indicated that someone besides him had found it. The Indians had no use for it; some probably heard of it, but few actually knew its location. It was a bad place to them, a place of the dead, best left alone. At least he knew they had not disturbed it, for the gold cross and iron case were intact when he found them.

Enough of this day dreaming Vincent thought. Work had to be done. They quickly organized the tack, rounded up their horses, and were on their way. They would be at Ft. Apache by nightfall.

Hector Antonne grew impatient with this extra delay. Brought on by Vincent Miles. He had not seen the Indian named Quintero again. This disturbed him as well. He had hoped to gain his service.

Perhaps, misfortune had befallen Vincent in his search for his Indian woman. "Tomorrow, I must make my departure," he said to himself.

His provisions were purchased and packed. Hector grew restless as the afternoon approached. At a distance he could see a man of Vincent's appearance. A second horse and rider followed. As they grew closer, Hector Antonne could see it was indeed Vincent.

"Señor!" He said loudly, as Vincent and the woman stopped by the porch he was sitting on. "Two days and more is a long wait. Perhaps you have trouble, eh!"

"The trouble is love, Señor Hector," Vincent said, as he nodded towards his woman. "You see, my friend, love is one thing you get the farthest behind on and get caught up faster than anything else in the world. Now that I am caught up on love, I am reporting for work, Señor."

Hector smiled and pushed back his hat. As he stood up, he said, "Good. We leave at daybreak in the morning!"

Vincent Miles and his woman went inside, and took a room for the night. Vincent paid extra, as the locals were not allowed. Staying in hotels would be a new experience for them, he thought. This would be the first time he had slept in a real bed with her.

When they left for San Francisco, he would buy her some dresses, he thought. Sleep came early this night. A lot had happened the past few days.

THE SEARCH
Chapter 5

Quintero had been waiting high in the rock cliffs several miles from Ft. Apache. He would trail along and keep an eye on the Mexican and Vincent Miles. The days of waiting had been long. Quintero had offered cornmeal to the four directions and prayed for strength to do what he must do. Vincent Miles was now in the company of his wife's sister, a woman he had grown to care for. She had become involved in something that even he could not assure her safety. For he did not know to what lengths she would go, to help Vincent and the Mexican find gold and return it to Mexico.

As the sky separated itself from the darkness, the riders made their way up the trail headed north towards the Mogollon Rim. They passed Cooley's Ranch and continued on in haste. Hector Antonne was anxious, to say the least. Too much time had been wasted obtaining the necessary government documents. Then, trying to locate key landmarks on old maps was a tedious job. Hector was ready to put some miles between him and Ft. Apache; much time had been spent here. He also knew, from the soldiers that many families of Mormons from Utah were settling in the area he intended on searching; time was of essence.

If they found the cross first, his journey would be in vain. Once again, Hector scolded himself for letting doubt enter his thoughts. "Surely, God wishes this thing," he thought.

They spent the first night on the Mogollon Rim. Vincent Miles had surprised some turkeys in a meadow and downed one with his Winchester. On a fire of oak wood, it was roasted to a golden brown. Thus their evening took on an air of celebration.

Quintero continued along behind, trailing the group. He had no intention of letting any gold go to Mexico. It still made him uncomfortable that his wife's sister was involved in this. After all, it was he who helped get her through the great sadness and grief when her children died. Now, he was in a position that might force him to harm her, if necessary. Still his honor bound him to do what was necessary to stop them from taking gold from the earth. He would have to deal with this when the time came.

Quintero had not built any fires while waiting for Hector Antonne to leave Ft. Apache. He did not want smoke to give away his position. So, once again, his meal was venison jerky. Quintero had seen the iron cross the Mexican searched for. He and his wife and her sister had gone there, two falls back and hunted antelope. They had killed several, and dried their flesh on the banks of a creek nearby. They had ridden out to Vincent's camp to see if any sign showed he had used it recently. The woman wanted to know. It was at this time that he saw the cross. It was standing, slightly bent over, under a cedar tree. Fragments of bones littered the area around it. It was plain that Vincent had not been there for a long time. The woman left feeling sad, for her memories were still alive of him and this place.

"Let's leave now!" she said, as they rode away heading back to the creek they were camped on.

Quintero prayed to the Great Spirit long into the night.

As the sun began to lighten the horizon, he was ready at a moment's notice to move on. When he was sure the others had gone ahead, he continued. He waited for a while on a small incline to see that everyone was accounted for. He didn't want anyone circling back and discovering him.

As they passed the timberline, and began to drop down into the great cedar plains, they jumped a herd of elk. They watched them for awhile, and then continued on.

Hector Antonne had selected a spot on the maps at Ft. Apache that most closely matched the description of the location where Father Antonne left the "Cross of St. Stephen." It would be up to Vincent Miles to locate the place, and decide where to camp. From there, Hector planned on making day searches in every direction. This way, he planned on establishing the most comfortable camp possible. Food could be prepared more easily; shelter could be created to protect them from the elements. Hector did not know how long the search might go on, but he planned to make a complete search of the area.

Hector did not trust his guide, Vincent Miles. He had told him too much the first night they had met at Ft. Whipple. Now, here he was sharing what information that was left with him. It was an uneasy alliance.

Hector had hoped the big Indian named Quintero would be some help to him. He had a gut feeling as he talked to him, that he had touched some spot deep in his inner being, but to date, it was not so. The man, Quintero, had failed to return the next morning, or thereafter. Hector couldn't help but feel alone in this new land, a feeling no doubt familiar to Father Antonne of old.

Vincent noticed the uncanny ability Hector Antonne had for reading maps. The place where he wanted him to locate their camp was not far from the site of the iron cross. Vincent had hoped to make this search last for a month or two. This would enable him to draw enough funds for a grubstake. Vincent would need time to find a suitable buyer for the gold cross. All this could come to naught if Hector stumbled upon the iron cross to quickly. The case the gold cross was protected in for two hundred years. Hector would see the gold cross was gone. He might even suspect Vincent, but of course, would have no proof. He knew to be careful, or the plans he had for the future could fall apart like a house of cards. He even considered hiding the iron cross, but that, too, might harm his plans. No, he thought, best to just go through the motion and play ignorant. If Hector finds the iron cross, it will be on his own. Then he may have a feeling of accomplishment and go back to Mexico with it.

Hector was happy, to say the least, when they arrived at the selected camp spot. It turned out to be a better location than he expected. The view of the surrounding plains was breathtaking. Grass was as tall as the horses' bellies. Antelope grazed in two herds on the horizon. A small hill behind camp would offer some protection from the prevailing wind of the area. Best of all, the bog, his grandfather wrote about in his diary, lay below him. The stock could water there and camp water could be brought from the creek a short ride away. Yes, this place will work fine, he thought. Hector knew a lot must be done to establish camp as he wanted it, but he could not contain his enthusiasm for the search any longer. He gave the others instructions, and rode towards the valley that formed the bog.

Hector thought of Father Antonne, and marveled how far he had ventured from Mexico City, and the hardships he must have endured before his return. He got off his horse and walked, trying to get a feel of this place. The water was only potholed at the moment, but he could tell that in the rainy seasons, this place became a moving body of water. He followed the lowest point of the bog for some distance. The cross has to be here, close, he thought. Just before sundown, he rode back to camp. He felt like a new man. "Finally, finally!" he shouted to the others.

Quintero chose a spot across the valley to camp. He found a place where he could keep an eye on the others. He could also see Vincent Miles' old antelope hunting camp. From there, he hoped to wait and see who came up with what they were seeking. Then, his job would really begin, he thought to himself.

The days passed. Yet, no one traveled toward the antelope camp. Quintero busied himself making a medicine bag. He followed a strict regimen each day that he established for himself, all the while keeping an eye on the comings and goings across the valley.

In time, Hector Antonne broadened his search, while Vincent and the woman spent less time afield. To his way of thinking, this indicated that Vincent grew tired of the search, or of waiting. The moon was full. Quintero decided to make use of it, go over to the iron cross and look to see if it lay undisturbed. It took him awhile to find it at night, but soon he was on his knees under the cedar tree where the cross stood. He reached out and touched it. Then he pushed against it. It was loose! Quintero knew it had been disturbed recently. He pulled the iron cross from the earth. He could see it had fresh marks on it. Upon examining it, he could tell that the cross had been opened, exposing a cavity designed to hold something of great importance, something gold, for this is what the Mexicans and Whites hold most important. So, this is it, he thought. A gold cross was once in this case. Quintero returned the iron cross back to the way he found it. He dusted away his tracks and returned to his camp. As he lay on his brush mat, he pondered the events of this night. He now knew that Vincent most likely had the gold cross, but wondered why he didn't take it and run. He must have greater feelings for the woman than he had thought. Sleep did not come this night to Quintero. He felt the spirits were trying to tell him something, but he could not hear them.

Vincent grew tired of the search. A powerful thirst had been developing since he had left Ft. Apache. Hector had forbidden any "spirits" being taken with them. Vincent had obliged him, but now regretted not hiding a bottle in his bedroll. He had decided to act like he was going to range further out and spend the night on the trail, then return the following evening. He was actually planning on riding north to Horsehead Crossing, tie one on, and then bring back a couple of bottles for later.

When morning arrived, Hector saddled his horse, bid farewell to Vincent, then headed off in a course due for the iron cross. This unnerved Vincent for a moment, then his thoughts gained momentum,

"Perhaps this is the day," he said under his breath. "It's only a matter of time until he finds the iron cross. He's eliminated so much area he is bound to find it soon. He won't be expecting me for two days, plenty of time to get the jump on him." These thoughts continued as Hector approached the small rise where Vincent camped in the past. He began to feel uneasy inside.

"Yes, it's time to go!" Vincent decided. He did not want a confrontation. The cross would do no good if he was shot up or dead.

Vincent began to pack up his belongings, and told the woman to fetch the horses. He did one thing he had neglected for a while. That was to clean his weapons--rifle first, then his handgun. "Never know," he thought, as he polished them across his pant leg.

Vincent wanted to make sure Hector had time to make it past the iron cross before he left camp; not wanting to be disturbed at what he had to do now. He told the woman to wait in camp, then mounted his horse, and headed towards where the gold cross lay buried.

Quintero was watching Hector ride towards him. He saw him pass the old antelope camp without doing anything unusual. He was busily watching Hector, and almost failed to notice Vincent riding out of camp.

"The woman remains," he thought; "this in itself is unusual. They have stayed together at all times on this journey." Hector turned north a short way from the hill Quintero was on. As soon as he was out of sight, Quintero caught his mount and rode in the direction Vincent traveled. The distance was not far. Vincent dismounted and tied his horse to a cedar tree, then walked over to a sand hill and began to dig in the earth. In a short time, a blanket wrapped bundle appeared. Vincent quickly walked back to his horse and tied this bundle on. He was soon on his way back to camp. Quintero circled the trees and advanced slowly. He could see the woman also was mounted and ready to ride soon as her man returned. When Vincent reached her, he spoke for a moment, then they rode towards the west. Quintero froze where he was until they passed by him. He had no intentions of letting them get out of his sight.

STRANGERS IN CAMP
Chapter 6

Hector Antonne looked back towards camp, he saw a man approaching from the north. He was a stranger to him, probably one of the Mormons he had heard about. Hector was curious about these people. He was told they take several wives. "They must be very brave men to have more than one woman under the same roof," he thought. As the man came close, he spoke loudly to Hector.

"Good day to you, Brother."

"And to you, as well," Hector responded.

"I am searching for some lost cattle that strayed this past night," the stranger offered.

Hector countered, "I search for the Iron Cross."

The Mormon then said, "I walk by the iron rod as well," thinking he was a Catholic Priest.

"No, Señor!" Hector replied; "I search for an old iron cross erected in this land many years ago."

"I have heard of a gravesite close by with an iron cross on it. I have not seen it, but my children have. We figure it was left by Spanish explorers in the past."

"You figure right!" Señor Hector said.

"It is over that way," the farmer pointed.

Hector was barely able to contain his excitement as he bid farewell to his unknown benefactor. The stranger turned and rode towards the west. Before he got very far, Hector paused and called to the stranger:

"What are you calling your town?"

"Snowflake, brother!" he said with a smile on his face. He spurred his mount and was once more on his way.

Hector headed back almost the same way he had come earlier in the day. The direction the farmer pointed out was towards his camp. Hector rode slowly searching every thing in his path. He came to a small rise and noticed a circle of rocks where someone had camped in the past. He stopped and tied his horse to a cedar tree. He began to explore the surrounding area. After circling the campsite several times, he found a few small pieces of iron once belonging to a wagon. He dropped to his knees to scratch around in the earth for more pieces. It was then; he saw the iron cross under a nearby cedar tree. Hector's hands and legs trembled as he crawled under the tree. He paused a moment, and reached for the cross. His hands ran the length and width of the iron cross.

"So long I have waited!" he said out loud to himself.

Next, he pulled gently on the cross. He did not expect it to move so easily. He pulled once again firmly and the cross came out of the earth into his hands.

In a moment, the iron cross lay opened on the ground, exposing its emptiness. The disappointment was overwhelming. Hector clutched his stomach, and bent forward in anguish. It was obvious to him that someone had recently been here, for the scratches revealed that. Also, by removing the loose dirt from the hole surrounding the cross, Hector could see that something once extended deeper into the earth.

"The Gold Cross of St. Stephen!" he said to himself.

At once a rage engulfed him.

"Vincent Miles!" he said. "Vincent's done this!"

Hector returned the iron cross to its former position and ran for his horse. In a moment, he was racing back to where he had last seen Vincent Miles. Upon reaching camp, he could see Vincent had packed his gear and pulled out. He grabbed some provisions and began to follow the fresh tracks. He discovered where Vincent had left camp by himself and trailed him to where he had hidden something, most likely the gold cross, Hector thought. He then followed Vincent's tracks back to camp where he and the woman both left together. Hector knew he only had himself to blame, for it was his whiskey mouth that caused all this trouble. Hector could not believe 'the luck' he had. Only chance brought them together that night, someone that was familiar with the area he was planning on searching. "The whiskey, damn the whiskey," he thought.

He had not gone far when he came upon a third set of hoof prints. Perhaps the farmer, he thought. Soon though, it became apparent someone was following Vincent, for when his tracks stopped so did the third party. "This is getting more complicated," thought Hector. Still he pushed on quickly. If he did not retrieve the cross before it fell into another's hands, he might not be able to do so. The more who find out about the cross, the more impossible it becomes. He thought of his uncle in his old age back in Mexico City. He depended on Hector to bring the cross home so he could go to the land of the dead in peace. His whole family counted on him. Hector rode on. "Soon it would be dark," he thought. "The moon will be up, and full, perhaps they will ride on in the night," he reasoned. "No, most likely they will not," he concluded. "They planned on being gone two days at the morning meal. They figured they had that much time before I came looking for them," Hector settled on.

He could tell the tracks were getting fresh, so he began to be more cautious. From a hill above, he could smell the distinct aroma of cedar wood burning below. Vincent was not worried about being followed, Hector thought. He tied his horse, and proceeded on foot. He could hear voices sounding from the camp. He crawled on his belly to within sight of it. To his surprise, four men were busily preparing a meal around a fire. Hector retreated as best as he could before he alerted them of his presence. He decided he'd better go down hill to get away as fast as he could. Soon as he made the brush, he stood up and got his bearings. He was now below the rise and down a dry creek from his horse. These four men must have been coming from the opposite direction, he decided. Their tracks were not over Vincent's, so Vincent and the woman are here somewhere nearby, he reasoned.

Hector had not gone far when he saw the tracks he was searching for. They led into a blow down of scrub pines. Hector once again crawled low to the ground to get close to those he pursued. This time all was quiet. He saw the outline of the horses behind Vincent and the woman. A tiny fire burned, and they were gathered around it eating. Hector thought for a moment, as he examined the situation: "This man is more Indian than I realized."

Hector, gun in hand, raised up slightly and headed into the camp. A twig snapped. Vincent's eyes met Hector's. In a second or less, Vincent's pistol was out of its holster blazing a deadly burst of lead. Hector was slow to fire, and a bullet from Vincent's gun scored a hit to Hector's shoulder. The force of the impact threw him to the ground. He winced in pain. Vincent cursed him, as he crossed the few feet between them. He pulled the hammer back on his gun once again, planning on playing the deadly game that was in progress to its end.

From the darkness, a giant figure of a man was in camp among them. Vincent was unaware of his presence. He was focusing on Hector Antonne, lying on the ground. As the man came up behind Vincent, the woman let out a mournful sound. Vincent spun around to see why she was making such a noise. It was then he saw the Indian, Quintero, coming at him with his knife in his enormous hand. He raised his gun up to fire, as he pulled the trigger; the woman threw herself between them to protect her brother-in-law. She took the bullet from Vincent's gun, and collapsed in Quintero's arms. As quick as lightning, Quintero threw the body of the woman against Vincent, pushing him to the ground. Quintero leapt at him with deadly speed and buried his knife deeply in Vincent's chest. Vincent gasped for air as blood formed around the wound. He slumped over the closest saddle and died. Quintero next sized up the Mexican. He could see his gun lying far from him. For a moment, he considered killing him as well, and burying the cross of gold with him. This way it would be over. But he remembered the night at Ft. Apache when their spirits talked. He knew there was something unusual about this man. He next went to the woman lying on the ground. She had saved his life. Quintero listened at her breast for signs of life; there was no sound. She, too, like her man, was dead.

Quintero decided to let the Mexican live and looked after his wound. Quintero applied cloth to stop the bleeding. Next, he found the blanket-wrapped bundle and exposed the "Cross of St. Stephen." Hector's eyes teared as he looked upon the cross. Quintero turned the cross around and around by the small fire, marveling at its beauty. He discovered the threaded cap at the bottom of the cross and unscrewed it. Two bones fell into his hand, dropping them quickly, he asked, "what are these?"

"Those are the bones of St. Stephen," Hector replied. "They are sacred to my people."

"Are they of this man hanging on the cross?"

"No!" Hector replied. "That man is Jesus Christ, the Son of God."

"You say then that your people worship a dead God," questioned Quintero?

"No, but evil men did put Him to death," replied Hector.

Quintero thought about this for awhile, then said to Hector: "I will bury these bones here. Then this man's spirit will be free."

He took out his knife and dug a small hole in the ground near where he sat. Carefully he used his knife to scrape the bones into the hole, and covered them with earth. Next he took a small amount of cornmeal and sprinkled it over them.

Hector looked on in silence. He felt that danger had passed for the moment. If this giant man was going to kill him, he figured he would have done so by now. Quintero asked him about his horse, and wanted to know where he left it. Soon, he returned riding it into camp. Quintero shared what few scraps of food he had with Hector and made him a bed of saddle blankets that the cross was wrapped in.

Quintero worked hard into the night digging a hole large enough to bury the man, Vincent Miles, and the Indian woman. The woman, bound by both love and family ties, stepped between two men. Hoping to stop the obvious, that death was going to claim one of the men. In the end, it was her and her man that death chose. The woman forfeited her life to save that of her brother-in-law.

Quintero's heart cried out in sorrow for he, too, had feelings for the woman he buried this night.

After this task was completed, he rested.

The following morning, Quintero and Hector began the long journey back to his rancheria on the Salt River. Hector endured the pain as well as possible. They would stop and rest every couple of hours. At this time Quintero dressed Hector's wound with herbs found along the trail. The journey took three days, and upon completion, Hector was beginning to feel a little stronger. Yet, Quintero insisted he rest.

The golden cross remained hidden by Quintero. He would bring it out occasionally and question Hector about it. Foremost, he wondered why they would make such a thing to take among his Indian brothers, the Zuni. Hector did his best to answer the many questions. He told him the cross was a symbol of bringing their beliefs to the Indians, and to celebrate the Catholic belief in God. Quintero still had reservations of his own about the gold cross. To him, anything gold was bad. He had seen first hand what the Whites and Mexicans were willing to do for it. Yet, he began to feel that this was different.

Hector felt close to this giant red man. His strength returned, yet he lingered on, in the company of Quintero and his family. They hunted together for deer and turkey. They swam in the river behind his home. Most of all, though, Hector enjoyed the stories the Apache men gathered around and told. He learned first hand the tale the Navajos passed on to the Apaches about the escape of the Sly One, Father Hector Antonne, his ancestor. They would spend hours a day telling and retelling their history in story form.

When the days began to grow short, Hector knew it was time to return to his home in Mexico City. He approached Quintero and asked straight way if his red brother was going to allow him to return with the great "Cross of St. Stephen" to his people. Quintero looked down at the ground for awhile, then looked towards the sunset. He spoke about the need of all to have a belief in God.

"Yes," he said. "You may go."

Quintero left for a moment, then returned carrying the cross. He sat down and opened his medicine bag. He removed a small carved bear with a little eagle feather tied to its back. Hector had seen it before around the neck of the Apache woman who had saved Quintero's life. Quintero once again began to speak.

"If it were not for the woman who owned this, we would both be dead and the gold cross would be lost. It is, therefore, her life that returned this cross to you. I place this bear inside the space where the bones once were. I feed it cornmeal, to give life to her memory that it might live on. Always remember that the Indian people, who were meant to be saved by this cross, now return it. Go carefully, my brother."

Hector returned to his shelter and began to pack his few belongings. He admired the cross. Then, he returned it to the buckskin bag Quintero had made for this purpose. He fell asleep to Quintero's singing on the hill above the Salt River. Tomorrow, he would start his journey home.

HEADED HOME
Chapter 7

Hector rose before daylight the next morning anxious to ride for Mexico. He had slept little. So many things were on his mind; things of late, like Vincent Miles, the Apache woman, Quintero himself, to name a few. All of these people in one way or another helped make his trip to recover the Cross of St. Stephen a success. Now, as he prepared to ride out of Quintero's Rancheria on the banks of the Salt River, he was a different man than the one who left Mexico. For events that happened on the search had given him insight into a world before unknown.

Hector Antonne was surprised, when he walked to the corral to catch his horse, Quintero was already up and prepared to ride. Hector had supposed he had bid him farewell the night before. Quintero was in good spirits so he had not changed his mind about allowing him to ride out with the golden cross. Of this, Hector was relieved, for he needed no trouble with his enormous friend.

"Buenos Días, Señor Quintero," Hector said upon walking up to his friend.

Quintero smiled and pulled his horse toward the corral fence. "We ride soon, my friend," Quintero returned.

Hector's surprise showed upon his face.

Quintero only increased his smile. His white teeth shone brightly in the morning light. "My brother does not want company?"

"No, that is not the case at all!" Hector quickly came back. "I am just surprised that you would do this for me with winter at hand. I know you have a lot of preparation you must do before snowfall. It will be my great pleasure to have my red brother ride along with me. I have had some worry about traveling such a great distance by myself with the golden cross."

"Good. We go then," Quintero said.

They finished packing what belongings they were taking and mounted up.

Quintero yelled a loud goodbye to his family, and they splashed across the Salt River and headed south.

The two riders traveled down the military trail to the San Carlos River. At the village of Rice, they headed up the Gila River to the Santa Teresa Mountains. At Eagle Crossing, they entered Arivipa Canyon, then south to the Sulfur Springs Valley. Ft. Grant lay ahead. Quintero was back in his homeland, the land of his youth.

They had ridden hard for several days to get here. Now, Quintero wanted to show his Mexican brother some places important to him, before Hector crossed over into Mexico.

"Tonight, we sleep at Metate Mound," Quintero said.

They neared Ft. Grant and settled in a spot by a creek that came down from the sacred mountain.

"Melted snow!" Quintero said, as he stretched beside the stream and drank his fill.

Hector jumped down from his horse and did the same.

"My people came here forever," Quintero said as they sat around a small fire. "Before the long knives, this was a place they camped to harvest acorns. The best acorn stew was made here by my mother. Time has changed all of that. This land has been swept clean of my people. They were loaded up in boxcars like oxen and taken away by the soldiers. As far as I know, I alone am here today."

With that, Quintero rose and took out a leather bag. He walked off by himself and began to sing. He sprinkled corn meal as an offering. After sitting down, he watched the last sliver of sun being pushed aside by darkness.

Hector was sleeping when Quintero finally rose and walked over to him.

"We go," Quintero said; "the soldiers are not happy tonight. It's not safe to stay here."

Hector rubbed his eyes to clear his thoughts. He rose and caught his horse. They mounted and rode several more miles before coming to a small overhanging rock cliff in a sand wash. Quintero reigned in his horse and dismounted. Hector followed his lead. This time they did not bother to build a fire. Sleep soon found them both.

Hector Antonne woke as the light played across his face. He rose up and looked around. Quintero's horse was by his, but he could not see his friend anywhere. He walked out into the wash where he could get a better look around. As he turned to go back to the horses, he felt a small pebble strike him on the shoulder. Looking up, he saw Quintero above him in some rocks watching the desert beyond them. Quintero motioned for him to hide in the rocks, but come up to where he was. Upon reaching Quintero, he could see a column of dust reaching the sky. "Soldiers," is all Quintero offered.

"What does this mean?" Hector asked.

"Last night much commotion in the Fort. Shots were fired. Maybe the Apache Kid tried to steal the soldier's horses. It would not be good for them to find us. They might suspect us. Bad trouble," Quintero finished.

They carefully worked their way back down to the horses. When they rode, they made their way up secluded washes crossing through saddles and worked their way along out of view of the soldiers. Thus, by nightfall they overlooked the large playa in the Sulfur Springs Valley. Small ranches dotted the once open land. They rested there this night.

The next morning, they rode past a small settlement the Whites had built. Quintero marveled at the amount of white men that had taken over the once wide open and free land he called home. Now he, an outcast, could only weep inside for the changes were not to his liking.

They continued in a straight fashion towards the stronghold. His people came here to hold on to there past as long as they could. For time had run out, and the stronghold would only offer freedom a short season. Now only their dead remained in this sacred place.

Upon reaching the entrance to the stronghold, Quintero dismounted his horse and began to lead him. Hector followed suit. He knew Quintero was deeply moved by this place. Hector remained quiet out of respect. They rounded a small outcropping of rocks and came upon a grove of trees. Quintero dropped the horse's lead and let the animal wander off to eat. He then headed towards the trees. Hector followed along quietly.

Quintero spoke softly as he entered the grove of trees. "My father, look the other way. Yes, look the other way, my father. It is I, your son, Quintero. I alone wander this once great land of our people. I have continued in your quest to this very day as I promised you. No gold has left this sacred land with my approval. I have slain many men who tried to do so. Yet, this day a man with me takes a giant prayer stick of gold with him to Mexico. Inside it carries the bear of our clan and the Eagle feather to give it medicine and corn meal to feed them. Therefore, my father, look the other way as my Mexican brother passes through our once great land, the land of the Apache. He carries the Cross of St. Stephen. For one moment, forget the oath I promised you as he passes. Tomorrow will be as before, but this day look aside, my father."

Quintero began to sing a song, a song Hector had never heard. An emitence of pain was escaping his lips. He knew Quintero was mourning the loss of an entire race of people.

Hector quietly led the horses back the way they had come. He found water coming down a cliff from a spring above. It was here that he spread his blanket to rest. Quintero did not come into camp this night. He stayed at the grove of trees with his father. Hector did not bother him.

Hector woke up to the sound of Quintero calling to the horses. He quickly rose to his feet and walked over to him, whereupon he offered his hand in support. Quintero locked arms with him and pulled Hector to himself. "Ride on, my brother, ride in peace."

Hector looked once again into the eyes of his smiling friend. He saw good in this man with character far above the average. As he returned Quintero's smile, he said to his friend, "Ride in peace, my brother, ride in peace."

CHANGE IN PLANS
Chapter 8

"Look out!" Hector Antonne yelled as he spun around and fired into the outline of a man cloaked in darkness.

Quintero rolled on the earth until he found cover in some rocks beyond the reach of light produced by their campfire. Hector fired two more shots while fast on Quintero's heels. Silence followed the gun battle. The two men searched the darkness for intruders, would-be robbers who preyed on the travelers unlucky enough to cross their trail.

Quintero and Hector Antonne left the stronghold early in the day bound for the Mexican border. They had traveled easterly trying to stay to themselves. In the distance loomed the Chiricahua Mountains; they would follow them south to Mexico. Darkness found them, so they made camp in a big dry wash. While Quintero busied himself fixing something to eat, Hector Antonne buried the Cross of St. Stephen for safekeeping. They were eating when the first shot sounded. It just missed Hector's head and it sent his hat spiraling to earth.

Now they waited, hoping the bullets Hector fired found their mark. They didn't have long to wait; however, a sound caught Quintero's ear. A bandit was to his left drawing a bead on him with a pistol. A rock protected him except for part of his face and his gun. Quintero's knife found his hand and in one movement took flight towards the would-be assassin. Blood exited the wound the knife made in the man's head as his hand slumped to the ground, allowing the pistol to fall. Quintero retrieved the knife and spun around just as another shot was fired; he saw the flash of the discharged weapon. Once again his knife left his hand. This time into the darkness it went. He knew it found its mark by the sound of pain escaping dying lips.

He exercised extreme caution this time while retrieving his knife, not knowing if others awaited him in the shadows. Only silence prevailed, as he wiped the blood off his knife. He returned towards the rocks where his friend was when he last saw him. He found Hector slumped over, bleeding badly. He tried to talk but an eerie sound escaped from a wound in his chest. Quintero motioned for him to remain silent. He worked quickly trying to stop the bleeding. It was not to be. Hector died in his arms as the moon cleared Dos Cabezas.

Quintero could now see well enough to count the bodies of the bandits. He also found their horses hidden down the wash a distance; they totaled the same. For the first time since this deadly ordeal began, he took a deep breath. He exhaled and looked down upon his dead friend. The thought came to him that he did not know where Hector had buried the golden cross, the cross he now died for.

Morning came as Quintero was digging a grave for his friend to be buried in. He had decided in the night that it must not be the Creator's will for the cross to return to Mexico. Now, if he could find it, he would bury it with his friend. "Then it will be over," he thought.

The sun was well into its journey; still Quintero searched for the cross. Hector had hidden it well. He returned to the grave and piled dirt on top of his friend and wiped away all sign of digging.

He took the horses belonging to the thieves and Hector with him. The saddles were cut loose along the trail, away from the carnage behind him.

He would miss Hector. "More than a friend, a brother," Quintero thought as he rode towards home. Metate Mound lay ahead; he would rest there this night and ponder the events of late.

Steve Ivory paused for a minute. He had never quite grown accustomed to the confines of city life. He stared uneasily at the five men who joined him now at a saloon, in the town of Willcox, Arizona Territory. Cards were tossed and picked up intermittently by each of them. Some were tossed in disgust. Others were turned and displayed proving "lady luck" does smile on some.

Steve had held his own through the nightlong vigil. He had won a little money. It would give him a stake to keep him going. The day was getting started and people began to move on the street. Dogs barked as wagons rolled back and forth, getting too close to their watches. The morning bar people stopped by for an early mind set, before hurrying to their duties. All this did not go unnoticed by Steve.

A noise began to build in the corner of the room. Steve's boots clanked to the ground as he pulled them off the empty chair he had been resting them on. He stood up and meandered over to the growing crowd.

"An Indian just killed three men at Dos Cabezas. He robbed them and stole their horses as well. He was last seen riding toward the Indian Reservation," a man standing in the middle of the group said loudly.

The news caused quite a stir. Steve rubbed his chin in nervousness, like he always did. Coupled with the fact he had not slept all night made him rub it all the more. His hand went into his vest, his hand shook as he pulled out his watch--10: 00 a.m. Steve made a note. Not speaking to anyone, he left the saloon and headed up the road to the sheriff's office. Another crowd was building there. Eight men were deputized and were about to embark upon a chase, a manhunt. Steve eyed them over and figured they'd be lucky if the lone Indian didn't kill them all. They were mostly town folk who had never looked down the barrel of a gun aimed at them.

He talked briefly with the sheriff and found out what he knew about the crime.

"Seems the Indian missed one of the jaspers and he high tailed it to town. Said the Indian killed three of his friends. All were cowboys for an outfit over in New Mexico. They were heading into town for a whisky night," is all he said.

Steve didn't like this kind of thing happening in his "parts," a little Indian trouble he didn't need. People still were jumpy remembering the days Geronimo raided here.

He opened the door to his small home. It was actually a quarters adjoining the stables. A cat had somehow been locked inside and it hissed at him as it ran between his feet, exiting his digs. "Gol darn it!" Steve said as the cat scared him. He approached a bucket of water and poured some into a large bowl. He splashed the cool water upon his face. A mirror hung on the wall behind the wash bowl. One look convinced him why the cat had hissed at him. "You look foul!" Steve said to himself in disgust. "This city life is going to be your undoing!" he finished. For a moment, the thought entered his mind to shave, and then it left just as fast. Considering the shape he was in from being up all night, shaving was out of the question, he figured. A knot of hunger left a twisted feeling in his stomach. This sent an urgent message to his brain. He stumbled out the door and headed up the street to get a bite of food.

"Think you could wring a couple more eggs out of those chickens of yours?" Steve inquired.

The owner of the place smiled and said, "I already have. Had a feeling you might be in. But do you have any money left after that all night game?"

Steve didn't know the town's folk had taken such an interest in his poker game. He tried to ignore her. She had the spurs in and wasn't about to pull back.

"Well?" she said standing by the table next to him.

"Ah, Mary, I ain't looking for no grubstake; all I want is a couple eggs and toast. I've got money," Steve continued. "I won a small bundle!"

"Where there's a winner, Steve Ivory, there's a loser, don't you forget that!" Mary finished.

"Sound like my mother, Mary, instead of my cook!"

"Had you stayed around long enough to let her, I'm sure she'd have told you the same!"

"I'll remember that, Miss Mary. Now you go to fixing me some food!"

A cup of coffee filled his hands. He held it close and blew the steam from the top of the mug. "Hot!" he said as his mind worked at coming up with a plan. "A lone Indian who was able to kill three men with a knife. Sounds like Quintero. Not like him to do a messy job though and especially just to steal horses. Has to be more to this than that," he thought. Just then Mary returned with his eggs.

"Had some pork in the back, thought maybe you'd like some." The smile on her face betrayed that her tough image earlier was just a front.

"Thank you, ma'am!" Steve said.

Steve returned to the stable and saddled his horse. Ahead lay Dos Cabezas and perhaps, death. At least the unknown, Steve reasoned. Something about this ate at him. He knew Indians. He had lived side by side with them in the former wilds of a young Arizona. Now as civilization closed in on what was left, it made him and a few others search for pieces of a puzzle trying to find out what the true picture was going to look like. He always tried to second-guess his surroundings, never accepting them as they appeared, but searched for that little flaw that hid the obvious. Into this setting he quickly rode.

The tracks were marred by the posse who had arrived first. A campfire site was plainly visible, as well as other telltale signs. Two fresh graves stood south of the ring of rocks outlining the campfire. Yet, there was supposed to be three. Steve Ivory found a level piece of ground nearby and removed the saddle from his horse and stored it under a mesquite tree.

Quail called in the distance; Steve sat in the shade surveying his surroundings. He stood and walked over to the campsite. A feeling of death greeted him. It sent chills up his back. He shook himself and gained control of his thoughts. He saw where the many deputies had searched the area. "Too many tracks," he thought to himself. "They caused more harm than good." He began to search in circles around the camp, each one extending further from the fire pit. He had almost given up when he noticed a tattered piece of paper blown against a clump of cactus. He grabbed it and held it up to his face. "Looks like a important piece of writing," Steve thought as he rubbed his finger over an embossed section of the paper. Out of habit, Steve looked around to see if anyone was watching. He could not read, and it caused him great embarrassment. He folded the paper and quickly headed back to his horse. He thought it best to take the letter back to the only one he trusted well enough with his secret.

The distance yielded to Steve's swift horse and he was soon tying it to the hitching post in front of the cafe.

"Mary!" Steve called in a hushed tone. "Can I see you a minute?"

"What's the hurry, Steve?" she inquired. "Not like you to come right to the point so suddenly."

Steve produced the folded paper from his pocket and handed it to the woman. "Can you tell me what this says?"

Mary led him to the kitchen out of the prying eyes of her customers. "The light is better in the back," she said. She looked at the paper a moment, then began:

"To whom it may concern: Please extend Hector Antonne the needed help it might require for him to search the territory of Arizona, for a certain object of Antiquity. Extend to him a hand of friendship befitting of our Southern neighbor, the Republic of Mexico...

Acting Arizona Territorial Governor......Prescott, A.T."

She rubbed her fingers over the seal marks stamped into the paper. "This must be important!" she said as she looked at Steve.

"It might be," he said trying to down play the paper. "Don't tell anyone about this, Mary!" Steve said, more asking than telling.

"Where did you get this?" she asked.

"I found it out where the killing took place last night."

"Better get it straight over to the sheriff!" the woman said defensively.

"He ain't here. He is still out trying to trail the Indian," Steve finished.

Evening found Quintero sitting by a small fire at Metate Mound. His mind rehearsed the events that led to him being there. It was not until the following morning as he led his little band of horses away from the camp of death that claimed his friend that he saw the extra set of tracks leading away by themselves. "One man had left his 'friends to die. A cowardly act." Quintero thought. "The wrong man died at the Stone Heads."

Yet he knew the way of the Whites and Mexicans. This one would return with many. He was in danger at this very moment. "When the moon returns to this land, he would ride," he reasoned.

Quintero stood up and took a few steps to a stone nearby. "The stone of the ancients," he thought as he approached it. It was worn smooth by the many who sought it out. He found it comfortable, as he would seeing an old friend. He sang a song seeking strength to do what he must do, a song to keep alive that which was dying rapidly, a world that was familiar to a man like him who hung onto the past as an anchor to keep from being swept away by change. He stood up and reached into a leather bag. He found cornmeal and sprinkled it to the four directions.

Steve Ivory wasted no time getting on his way. Many miles now lay between him and his home. Something about the killing led him to believe more had happened than had met the eye. He had this gut feeling that drove him onward. Now a name on an official document lending mystery to this story had him confused. Still, he felt like part of the answer, or perhaps all of it, waited on the Indian Reservation ahead. His horse lathered as it pulled the hillside trail.

Darkness greeted him as he entered the military post of Ft. Apache. He sought audience with the post commander and received it. He asked specific questions about a man, a Mexican named Hector Antonne. A startled face betrayed the fact that the name was familiar to him.

"Mister Antonne, yes, he was here for a short while. A very short while, in fact. Why is it you seek him, Mr. Ivory?"

"My only interest in him is to solve a crime. Three murders were committed an eyewitness claims. Yet only two bodies were recovered. A piece of paper with his name on it was found close by."

"Then you are a lawman, Mr. Ivory?"

"No sir, I am not!" Steve replied.

"What is your interest then? Surely you must have a reason," the post commander said.

"A single Indian killed the men with a knife. The only Indian I know who is capable of doing this is a large man I have encountered in the wilds of this territory. His name is Quintero."

"I have heard allegations before of such feats by this man. Yet he remains a farmer and breeder of horses below here on the Salt River. Could this possibly be the same man? Surely you jest, Mr. Ivory."

Steve found himself rubbing his chin as he listened to this man discount one of the strongest men alive. He obviously knew a Quintero he did not. "It's not my purpose here to implicate the Indian in the crime, though I feel he is more than capable. I feel if it were he who was the guilty party, the one accusing would lie dead with the others. Just the same, I would like to speak with this man, Quintero."

"I see no harm in you talking with the man. Do you require an escort of some of my men?"

"No, that will not be necessary," Steve replied.

"What did the paper say about Mr. Antonne?" asked the commander.

"It was a letter of introduction from the governor of Arizona asking those encountered to help Hector Antonne recover a lost artifact," Steve explained.

"Yes, I saw the letter you mention. I let him study our maps, to aid him in his search."

"What was it he sought after?" Steve asked.

"As far as I know nobody was ever told. Rumors floated around about a Cross of some kind. But I dismissed them as fiction," the Major added.

Steve thanked him for his time and left the room. The air was brisk outside. He breathed deeply. "Fall is here!" he thought as he gained his horse.

Ahead was an Inn he had used before. He had not secured lodging earlier, so now he hoped a room would remain for him. He recalled the Major's words and shuffled them like a deck of cards in his mind. "How much of this man's words could be counted on?" he wondered. "Had Quintero remained all these years cloaked behind an outer appearance of a peaceful farmer as he enforced punishment on those who dared find gold on Apache Soil?" Yet he, Steve Ivory, must admit only rumors and speculation hinted of these claims. No solid proof existed. No victims lived to press charges against the Indian.

A room was waiting for him, the first he had since leaving Willcox several days earlier. The night was short and filled with anxiety, so he awoke feeling tired. He had asked the innkeeper how to find this man Quintero. The man gave him directions as best he could. Now, as he rode above the cliffs looking down on the Whiteriver, he marveled of the beautiful surroundings. When the White and Black rivers meet it becomes the Salt River. "Beyond this point in a small canyon is the Quintero Rancheria," he had said. Steve watched his backside as he continued down the trail. Resentment still ran high on both sides of the reservation line.

Quintero heard the dogs bark outside his house. He lay inside resting the afternoon away. He had planned on leaving early the next day to hunt turkeys so he was "storing some rest," he told his family. Outside, the barking grew louder. A voice called out, one not familiar to him.

"Is this the house of Quintero?"

Quintero came close to the door and answered, "Yes! Who asks?" He then slipped quietly out the back door and crept around the corner of the house putting him within range of a knife blade if needs be.

"I am Quintero!" he said as he turned the corner.

Steve noticed how easily the Indian materialized to his left. "I would like an audience with you," Steve said.

"What is it that brings you here?" Quintero wanted to know.

Steve saw the giant Indian sizing him up, looking behind him to search the horizon, wanting to know if he was alone. Finally, content in the fact he was, he let his eyes settle on Steve's for a moment. Then his eyes avoided Steve's, as he continued the conversation.

"I am looking for a man named Hector Antonne." Quintero did not look surprised at the question, Steve figured.

"A good friend, he stayed with me here at my rancheria for awhile," said Quintero.

"I have reason to believe he was ambushed down by Dos Cabezas," Steve offered.

"So you are the law then?" Quintero asked.

"No sir, I am not," Steve countered.

"Then what?" Quintero asked letting his eyes once again meet Steve's.

Quintero took refuge in silence as he held his gaze. After several attempts, Steve finally got the red man to speak.

"You seek the Yellow Metal, don't you?" asked Quintero.

Steve, now on the defensive, raised his voice and defended himself from the truth. Quintero blushed with anger as he listened to Steve's words.

"Now hang on there a minute!" Steve interjected. "I ain't here trying to steal someone's gold. I just wanted to know what this man was doing up here looking for treasure."

"I have seen your eyes somewhere, in the past perhaps?" Quintero asked. "I have seen you up on the Blue, many seasons ago."

"Yes, we have cut trail before up there," Steve volunteered.

"But you were called something besides Steve Ivory. What was it?" Quintero wanted to know.

Steve stammered around for a minute, then spit out, "Lucky."

"Yes, you were the Lucky Boy, weren't you? I saw you there looking for gold. Did you find any? No, of course not; it is not there," Quintero said. "You can save that for someone else, Quintero. I know better. That jackass load of gold didn't come from too far from where I found it," said Steve

"Perhaps you're right then," Quintero replied; "you be the judge. So what would you have me do for you, Steve, or Lucky if you prefer?"

"Just call me Steve! Tell me about the night of the killings by Dos Cabezas."

"Hector and I had ridden all day and made camp early. I was fixing some food and didn't pay a lot of attention to what Hector was doing. He buried the cross for safe keeping."

"So you did have this cross that he searched for with you?"

"Yes, we did!" Quintero continued. "We had not seen anyone else all day, we became lax and let the bandits get the jump on us. They waited until dark and surprised us. Hector was shot through with a rifle ball. He bled to death in my arms. I buried him and scattered the extra dirt so nobody would find his remains and disturb them. The cross he came to find is now lost somewhere in the vicinity of Dos Cabezas. I did not know the cowardly bandit escaped until the following day. Otherwise, I would have followed him and took care of him as well."

"I never figured you to let gold leave the land of the Apache," Steve said.

"This was different, it was gold that came here from Mexico, gold that meant something other than lust for riches." Quintero tired of this conversation and started to return to his home.

Steve knew his audience with the Indian had ended. "One last thing before you go," Steve said. "Is the Lucky Boy Mine by Grasshopper Saddle?"

"A mine is where you find it. I thought the Lucky Boy was no more," Quintero replied. He turned and entered his home.

Steve Ivory entered Wilcox to find the population had returned to normal. "The routines of each, once more became the chains that bound them," he thought.

Steve Ivory had spent many days in search of the cross Hector Antonne had hidden by Dos Cabezas. "The bandits must not of found it," he reasoned, "or the remaining one would have taken the cross and high tailed it. No, the cross is still out their some place," he figured.

Mary fixed a lunch, and she and Steve went to Dos Cabezas for an outing. It had been bothering him for a while that he had spent his life by himself. He longed for a family to settle down with.

"Mary, this old cowboy has finally figured out there is something out there more important than gold. It's here with me today. I want to share it with you."

"And just what is that, Steve Ivory?" she asked. "Have you found the missing cross?"

"No, it's love," Steve said, looking at the ground, avoiding eye contact.

"Steve Ivory, look at me. Are you saying what I think you're saying? You are, aren't you!"

Steve smiled, "Well, what do you think, Miss Mary?"

"I think that would just be alright!" she finished.

Time builds. Time destroys. It never sits still.

"Steve Ivory!" a voice from behind him called out. "There's a man at the train depot looking for a guide to take him out to Dos Cabezas. Seems he's here to find out about his nephew's death a while back. Name's Señor Antonne. Think you could take him out there. Say's he'll pay in gold coin!"

Steve could tell the man from the rest of the people at the depot because of his appearance. He looked like a dandy. "Quite the dresser!" Steve said to himself. He rubbed his chin as he walked closer.

"Señor Antonne, I am Steve Ivory. I was sent to be your guide." "How long will we be out there?" he asked.

"Who knows, only God," said Señor Antonne.

"Spend the night at the hotel on Railroad Avenue and I will be outfitted and ready to ride in the morning," said Steve.

"Splendid! Señor Ivory, I will see you in the morning then?"

"Yes, you will!" Steve replied as they walked back in the direction he came from.

They reached the campsite they sought at 11:00 a.m. Steve set up camp and cared for the horses. Señor Antonne walked the area getting a feel of the land. "I feel death here, Señor Ivory!"

"I felt the same the first time I came here."

"Then, you have been here often?"

"Yes, Señor, I must admit, I have. I want you to have this. As far as I know it is all that remains of your nephew's possessions. I found it blown against a cactus over there." He pointed.

"Then, Señor Ivory, you must know about his search?"

"Yes, I do! Señor Antonne, the only part I'm unsure of is the cross," said Steve."

"What do you mean, Señor Steve?"

"I know it is gold. Is it large? Where did it come from?"

"I see you are full of questions, yet so am I. Perhaps, we can be of service to each other. First, though, my question to you is, does the cross remain here, or did someone recover it?"

"As far as I know, it is lost somewhere close by. I have searched repeatedly and been unsuccessful," answered Steve.

"I can see many holes dug here, Señor Ivory, yet you say the cross remains? Then the cross must be protected by the lives of the saints!"

"What do you mean, Señor Antonne?"

"Just that. I will be staying awhile," replied Señor Antonne.

Steve remained a few days, then drew his pay. Señor Antonne continued on searching for the golden cross. The 'Cross of Saint Stephen,' he called it.

"Home so soon?" Mary asked as he entered the kitchen.

"The ground grows harder each passing year," he told her.

"Never knew you to give up so easy on a search for gold," Mary said with a laugh.

"I have riches here at home, now!" he said as he held her close.

Two young boys came running through the doorway and pushed them aside. Steve and Mary stepped back and let them rush by.

"Fine boys, Mr. Ivory!" Mary said.

"Yes," Steve agreed proudly.

Steve Ivory awoke to the sound of his dog barking. Out of habit he got up and went and checked the locked doors. They remained as he had left them. He peered out the window and saw nothing unusual. He returned to his bed. Mary continued her normal rhythm of breathing. His eyes remained alert, even though the clock hands were busy.

The missing grave of Hector Antonne still bothered him. Without it, nothing placed Hector or the Indian Quintero at the site of the killing. And without Hector Antonne, the golden cross could not be placed there either. Other than the fact that Quintero had admitted to him that they were there, no proof existed to this except for a single piece of paper. It made finding the grave vital to determine what happened to the cross. Steve rubbed his chin as he thought. "Quintero! That's it, Quintero! He only said he buried Hector Antonne, he did not say where. He also said he had decided it was not the Creator's will for the cross to go to Mexico. Most likely he buried his friend and the cross together someplace other than where the killing took place. He said he wanted the body not to be disturbed."

A rooster crowed outside signaling a new day was about to begin. Steve looked out the window onto the street. People moved about on the sidewalk going here and there. "The cross must be buried with Hector Antonne!" Steve rubbed his tired eyes as the sun once again returned to claim its place in the western sky.

A CHANGE IN THE WIND
Chapter 9

"Like the black oak that grows on the lower slopes of the forest, it being a smaller tree, nonetheless, having the greatest strength. You, like it, my grandson, will be strong and do much good for our people. You will be one of the great ones like Naiche, Victorio and Juh; all were keepers of the secrets, the places of the Yellow Metal, where it rises to the sky. It is for us to hide it to keep our lands safe."

"Your father also kept the secrets and since he died young, I have raised you your entire life to take my place when the time comes. I have instructed your spirit as well as taught you the art of battle. You strike as the Jaguar. You have the strength of the Bear. The patience of the Lion. The stamina of the Horse."

"Grandfather, why are you telling me these things?"

"Little Bear, I feel the day is at hand when you shall ride in the lead. You have the swiftest horse. Ride fast, my son." Quintero turned to walk away from his grandson.

"Would my grandfather not see it to the end? Would the years that brought gray to his hair also blind his eyes? Have you grown tired of the battle? Does not each new day bring warmth? Does not love warm your nights any longer? Do all these things trouble you, grandfather?" asked Little Bear.

"The seasons hang heavy on my frame like a tree covered with snow. I have tasted the blade, and received lead more than once, yet I have prevailed. Many men have I sent across the barrier of here and there. I do not forsake my promise. Only now, I enter a time where you, Little Bear, will take the lead."

"If that day is here I will take your name, grandfather! Quintero will be on the lips of those who talk of gold. I will keep your name alive and your memory will ride with me forever," said Little Bear solemnly.

"It is well, my grandson, that you do this. I will be in the breeze as it blows against your face. I will be in the clouds that bring the first rain. I will be at your side if you need me. Now go, my son; we have talked enough."

This day brought a change, a change from the old to the new, from Quintero to his grandson, Little Bear, who would take the name Quintero while he kept the secrets.

Quintero rode hard hoping to make it back to his grandfather's Rancheria before nightfall. He had been gone for several months. He had found a mine he had never seen before. Two men worked it for a long period of time. It was very close to the mine of the Dutchman. He surprised them one morning as they left their quarters to relieve themselves. He killed them both and put them inside the mine and sealed it up. He was anxious to tell his grandfather about his trip.

The dogs barked loudly as he rode into his home.

"Little Bear, sit and eat with us," his grandfather offered. "How did you find things, my son?"

"I traveled down the Salt River to the Superstition Mountains. There I destroyed a working mine. After that I rode through the Pinals, and followed the Gila River to the San Francisco River, then up the Blue River. All the places remain secret. I encountered many Whites on the move. But they were not looking for Yellow Metal. Rain had uncovered the bed of nuggets the Whites call Adam's Digs, but I hauled in more earth to hide them," responded Little Bear.

"You have done well. What are your plans now?" Quintero inquired.

"I will round up my herd of horses and bring them in to winter here," Little Bear answered.

"Good, I will go with you," Quintero replied.

After they ate, they sat across the fire from one another. A pipe was filled with fresh tobacco and passed back and forth. In due time the grandson broke the silence. "Grandfather, what happened that seemed to change you?"

"I have not changed, I just came to realize my senses are not as sharp as before. I entered a trap set by bandits and was none the wiser. It cost my friend, Hector Antonne, his life. I also lost the golden cross and the stone bear and eagle feather I put inside it. The stone bear once hung around the neck of a woman special to me. It is those things that weigh heavy on my mind. If the golden cross is found, put it in the Old Mission Mine along with the chests of Spanish gold. It will be safe there. Bring the stone Bear to me."

Steve Ivory stayed clear of the poker games since he and Mary became husband and wife. She continued to run her restaurant down by the Railroad Depot. He tried working there as well, but the walls closed in on him to tight. He needed the outdoors to feel alive. He alternated between the Willcox Land and Cattle Co., punching cattle and stealing away searching for gold. He found a strike or two, yet the big one always eluded him.

"It is a disease," Mary had told him, as he rode off the last time. His boys watched as their father mounted his horse. They clamored to go with him, but their mother protested.

"You aren't teaching them to run around searching for gold," she said.

He longed to find "one more," just to prove to the unbelievers he could.

Ahead lay the Devil's Backbone, an unruly piece of real estate if he had ever seen one. He would be searching for mavericks for a few days. A vein of quartz ran through a ledge close to the trail. It caught his attention and he pulled up his horse. He bailed off and took his small pick to knock off a sample. "There's no hiding what my priorities are," Steve thought. "One more place I won't have to check again," he grumbled as he climbed back upon his horse.

The line shack would be home for a few days. He lay on a small cot in the corner of the single room building. He could hear the wind picking up outside. "It's going to get cold," he thought as his mind wandered in the space of in-between sleep and consciousness. "The Cross of St. Stephen, Quintero, Hector Antonne, how, where?" he thought, just as his snoring woke him up. He got up and tossed a few more sticks in the stove. "Well!" he said loudly to himself. "Better get some sleep; long day tomorrow."

THE THREE SISTERS' MINE
Chapter 10

Three friends sat in a tavern in Ireland. Three boys sat as boys will when they come of age. They had returned three lovely lasses to their home several hours ago. Now the bartender sat up drinks for the three lads, just as he had years before for the fathers of the three. A rite of passage transpired this night. No one would ever know except those in the room. --Three lads and an old barkeep blind in one eye from fighting the Brits.

The lads had nothing in common except one thing. They loved three sisters; three red headed girls, all beauties everyone. Each raised to be ladies, prim and proper. The barkeep knew better than to talk, for this was a night for listening. Each young man stood and told of his love, how he would one day seek his lady's hand and how his fortune would be made through hard work. He would do all this and more. Had not his father done this very thing before him? His mother's hand was secured by his father's cunning in battle with the English. Thus, he would somehow win his love's hand as well.

Times were hard. The potato famines raged. Every day people starved to death. Families were immigrating to the Americas in masses. Gold had been discovered in California. Tales of wealth hung on everyone's lips.

"Gold! Gold!" one of the lads shouted as he raised his mug, ale sloshing over the side. "Let us go there and make our fortunes!" he shouted.

One said, "We cannot go and leave our parents to fend for themselves. Times are too hard."

"You know as well as I that we would be doing them a favor to leave!" another shouted back. "They would have one less mouth to feed. We all have brothers and sisters to help them in our absence. I say we go!"

The three friends toasted each other, toasted their three loves, then finally they saluted and one said:

"For our love of three sisters, we go."

They all joined in and stood and repeated the toast, "For the love of three sisters, we'll go!

"It is set then. We will seek passage on the first ship bound for the California's on which we can work for passage," one offered.

Once again, they saluted.

It was a short night for the three friends. By the time they had reached home, it was almost time to rise and began the daily chores. They went through the motions, trying to act as if nothing was wrong. But it was obvious to them they were a mess.

Noon found them at the shipyard exploring what opportunity, if any, existed to get them underway. It was determined that a ship was bound for California in two weeks. In the meantime, a lot had to be done to prepare for such an adventure. They secured an oath from the three sisters not to betray them and tell their parents what they planned on doing. That night once again found them down at the local pub. The girls had been returned to their home. The young men's dreams once again soared.

The old bar keep swabbed the bar with a white rag. As he passed the three lads, he said loudly. "Fools, all of you. Yes, fools ye be!"

The lads lost their determination for a minute. All focused their attention on the old one-eyed dredge.

The barkeep kept working his way down the bar. "Fools ye be!" he said. "Yes, fools ye be. The fires of love grow cold, when the flames are not fanned!"

The three grew silent for a moment. Finally, one spoke for the three. "What do you mean, old man?"

"I mean while you three blokes are over scrambling through the hills of California, young Chatworth and the likes will be shining up to your girls. Aye, he will, or another, says I."

"The barkeep is right," said one of the lads.

"So he may be, but what choice do we have? To stay here is to admit defeat. We have no way to support nary a one of them. We must go and return with enough gold to win their fathers over. I say we go! Yes, for the love of three sisters we go!"

Three lads once again stood to toast their determination to proceed with their plans.

The ship would dock in one week and then secure its load headed for the Americas. Once there, it would deliver its goods at Boston, then set sail with cargo bound for California. A notice at the harbor announced a few job openings on a passage for work basis. They would be at the dock early enough to win a position for each of them.

So that's exactly what they did. After a tearful good bye, the three lads found themselves on the high seas headed for a new land they knew little about.

These young men were farmers and sheepherders. The ways of the sea was new to them; hard work was their lot. The deck hands knew of their ignorance and used it to their best advantage to extract extra work from them to lighten their own load, of course. Thus, the voyage was spent with them being virtually in bondage and working as if they were indentured, for indeed, that is what they were, in debt for the passage to the Americas.

Nighttime found them gathered around, lending each other support. Their boyhood was left upon that voyage somewhere in the Atlantic Ocean. For upon the vessel putting into port in Boston, three men disembarked. The roughness of the seamen had polished them into such. They had decided they could not endure the conditions on this ship any longer. They would stay in port and wait for a situation to open where they could continue on.

They found Boston almost as bad as being on the ship. So many Irish had emigrated in such a short time that they could not accommodate such an influx. Jobs were almost nonexistent and the three arrivals realized promptly that perhaps they had exercised poor judgment.

They, in time, found work on a fishing boat that was sailing up and down the coast. And while thus employed, they were able to win the friendship of several men who were instrumental in helping them gain passage on a working vessel bound for California.

They were, therefore, on the way once again. This time, at least, the captain and crew were honorable men. They had a job to do and that was all that was expected of them. They made their way down the coast of the United States, on to Havana, Cuba, then across to Panama. They took a pack train of mules up over the mountains and down to the Pacific Ocean where they boarded a ship and sailed north to the Californias. They found port at San Francisco, a thriving place made rich by the recent abundance of gold flowing into it.

Since the discovery of gold, the towns had emptied of men. All had left for the gold fields. Workers were in demand. It was easy for the three friends to find jobs. A dry goods store hired all three of them. They started with nothing, as they only had the clothes on their backs upon arriving in San Francisco.

They worked for two months before the combined wages of the three would outfit one of them to begin prospecting. They drew lots to decide who would be that one. Each was anxious to go, but fate only smiled on one for the moment. They had learned much from talking to the miners as they came into the store. It was decided by the three where they would send the appointed friend. It would be some time before they would see each other again, as the gold fields were several days journey on foot from where the two would continue to work. They planned on meeting again in two months to see if one more of the friends could be grubstaked by then.

So it was. The two friends continued on at the dry goods store hoping the other friend would strike it big and expedite the day when they would begin the search for gold.

As time wore on, the three lived for word from home. Three sisters were they--the boys' lives, their loves. Irish roses: the prettiest of them all. Yet they seldom received letters from them. The men grew to live by faith in what they were doing, for to many miles, yes, oceans separated them. But yet the girls were as close as their hearts. This love drove them on.

Two months came and went. The third friend found no gold. He needed another grubstake to continue searching. The other two Irishmen worked on at the store.

It soon became apparent to the two that more money was being made by the merchants than by most of the miners. The miners that struck it rich spent their earnings on drink and gambling. The rest went in the hands of the shopkeepers for supplies. The miners mostly knew a life of toil and hard living. This did not go unnoticed; they began to plan for a way to go into business for themselves.

The Irishmen approached their employer with an offer; they would take his merchandise to the biggest mining camps and reach customers he had no opportunity to sell to. The merchant had grown close to the three Irishmen and saw a chance to help them and increase his earnings as well. A deal was struck. The two friends would start immediately. They were outfitted with a large wagon and team. It was loaded with food, tools, and clothing. Just about everything they sold at the store was represented. Their employer took the two friends to the edge of town. He reached into a buckskin case and produced a sawed off shotgun.

"Ever shot one of these?" he asked.

The two friends shook their heads.

"Give her a try!" he said as he passed the gun to the closest man. "You'll be carrying a lot of gold dust as you sell these wares. I don't want any harm to come to it, or you," he said. "Usually a man will run from just a look at a double barrel aimed their way. Shoot at that rock over yonder," he added.

They enjoyed this, the sound, the smell of the black powder burning. The excitement brought them to life. Hope for the future, the love of three sisters once more drove them onward. They hoped to explore this big new country, find their other friend and, perhaps, find the wealth they needed, the wealth to return home, to seek out the hands of their loves.

Daylight found them rolling down the road in the new wagon. They never traveled far without opportunity presenting itself to stop and sell some of the goods they carried. The first mining camp they arrived at consisted of many bars and gambling halls, but no mercantile stores. Probably eight hundred men worked in this vicinity. The goods were all sold. They cleaned them out before the sun went down. They hurried back for another load, and another. It finally looked like they were on the right track. The third friend still had not located a substantial amount of gold so he joined them in selling goods to the miners. They now started a new approach. Two of them would stay at a mining camp and sell out of a tent while the other one returned for a new load. When sales began to fall, they would move on to another camp.

The gold dust began to pile up in the safe in the dry goods store's back room. The twenty five percent of the profits that was their share would soon be enough for them to return to Ireland and ask for the sisters' hands in marriage. Then hopefully they could return and continue on with the lucrative business they were engaged in.

One night, while they were out selling at a distant mining camp, tragedy struck. A fire consumed the dry goods store and all its contents. The proprietor, their partner, lost everything. Some say the fire was started to cover a robbery of the gold from the safe in the back room. No sign of the gold, molten or otherwise, was ever recovered. The partner was devastated. The only thing left was the team and wagon and what goods were in it. It was given to the Irishmen to settle for part of the gold that was theirs. The rest they lost as well.

By this time, gold was being found further and further up in the Sierras. The three went to various gold fields and tried prospecting, only to have luck pass them by. The better areas were worked out and many miners were beginning to form a reverse gold rush; that is, prospect the streams and mountains of Nevada, Arizona, Colorado, and New Mexico, places passed up as everyone raced to California. The friends first went over the Sierras to Virginia City and Carson City, Nevada. Once again, they found more money in hauling freight than in digging gold. They took turns keeping the team and wagon making a profit for them, while the other two searched for a strike in gold or silver. It was not to be; luck ignored them.

Next, they put the wagon to work on various claims in the desert of Southern California, hauling supplies to the mines there on contract. Two of the friends would stay behind and work for wages, while the other one drove the wagon. Word reached them of a fabulous silver strike in Southern Arizona, at Tombstone, so they decided to move on in that direction.

They fared better than some. They had the team and wagon and some gold they had saved. Mainly, though, it was the experience they gained that mattered. They had been in the mining districts long enough now that they knew as much about mining as anyone. They just could not find "that right place."

They crossed the desert to Yuma and prospected there for gold a little while. Then they proceeded on to Tucson. Next, they went east to the San Pedro River and followed it southward towards Tombstone, joining others in search of wealth. With this influx, the population soared, making it the largest town in the area. Most, like them, only found disappointment.

They decided to move further away from the crowd. North and easterly led them to a series of small mountain ranges, lying one after another. They traveled onward; always prospecting each outcropping of rocks and panning likely looking washes. They passed the large playa that seemed to go on forever. They headed north from here prospecting as they went.

They could tell they were being watched by Indians. They had seen them from a distance but they appeared to be uninterested in them. They had been warned when they left Tombstone to beware, so they carried weapons and were ever on the defensive.

They found a canyon with abundant water. There they camped and worked the area. Samples were brought in each day and crushed and panned out in a pool of water. Small amounts of color were found but not enough was recovered to warrant full scale mining.

All of this changed one day in the fall. The weather had begun to show some signs of cooling down. Two of the friends had crossed over a couple of ridges from camp. High on one of these ridges, a small outcropping of rocks appeared interesting. They walked over to it for a "look and see." They picked at the rocks and broke several into small pieces. They could see flakes of gold in the rocks. They hurried back to camp with these samples. After crushing and panning them out, a good portion of gold remained in the pan, the best they had found so far.

That night, a small celebration was held among the three friends. They cooked some deer meat, biscuits and gravy. After they had eaten, one of them produced a bottle that had been hidden under the seat of their wagon for just such an occasion. He filled three tin cups, then raised his drink in a toast.

"This seems to be it, lads, what we've searched for so long and hard. The vein goes into the ground, the samples are good. I name this mine after our three loves at home in Ireland. I name it the Three Sisters' Mine."

"Salute," they all yelled as they downed the toast.

They finished off the bottle that night.

The next day found them back up on the ridge working the vein. It went down the face of rock. They continued crushing samples and testing them. Each sample contained gold!

The three friends were excited. Once again, they could think of the plans they had made and work towards them. Three sisters were on the minds of the three friends. Gold is what they needed to make there plans work. The gold recovered would buy the tools; powder and equipment needed to dig a shaft to follow the gold bearing vein. This was lode gold in hard rock; it would be challenging but the stakes were high. The three friends gave it their all. A shaft was opened around the vein of ore. It went straight down in the hard rock. The strike was not the richest mine in the country, but at times it paid well.

The gold they recovered was hidden in a hollow oak tree north of camp. It was easy to hide it there because solid rock lined the creek it grew by, thus enabling them to walk to it without leaving footprints. Soon, they had extra funds needed to build a suitable house to live in. A stable was erected also to house the stock. A small barn was finished and filled with hay.

The Indians were always present, but were reclusive. The three friends knew they came at night and gathered up the turquoise they were blasting out of the mine. A small amount of it was mixed with the ore containing gold.

Then, as time passed, the Indians became more visible. Sometimes the women would come over from Apache Canyon where they camped during the day and look over the tailings. The three friends always saved a few of the better pieces of turquoise in case they needed them to barter with. They knew deer and turkeys could be purchased with the blue stone. The red men placed more value on it than gold.

The Irishmen marveled at the difference between themselves and the savages, native to this rugged land, a land that would kill with no remorse. The Irishmen now claimed this land as their home. Ireland retreated back to a place in their memory, a place where three sisters lived, as well as Mom, and Pop, brothers and sisters. But they lived in this rough and rugged land, shared with the red men. Yes, they were lucky for having the blue stone in the mine; otherwise, the Indians would not be so tolerant.

At a hundred and twenty five feet, the vein drifted. The blue stone stopped and no longer was mixed with the ore containing gold. They knocked pieces off when they could on the way up from the mine. They left them where the Indians could find it easily.

Juniper timbers were cut from the mountains above the mine. One of the friends would take the wagon and team, go up, and stay until a load was cut. Usually it would take several days. But it was a welcome change from working long hours in the mine. From such a trip, one of the Irishmen was overdue. The two friends began to worry that perhaps trouble had found him. At first light, they started the ascent up the mountain in search of their friend. They trailed the wagon to where it was stopped. The horses were still in harness but there was no sign of their partner. After searching, they found where he had been attacked while returning home. Several Indians had surrounded him. He had retreated to some rocks where he had held them off for awhile, but to no avail. The Indians overpowered him and shot several arrows in him.

From high on the side of the mountain where they found their friend, they could see the dust of several riders on the desert floor below them.

"The Indians," one friend yelled, "who probably did this, are leaving Apache Canyon, most likely some we know. What a shame lad, what a shame. If we only could have helped him."

"At least they didn't kill the horses," one of the friends spoke under his breath.

"Let's take him to the wagon and head home," the other one said as he turned away so his fellow Irishman would not see the tears filling his eyes.

A grave was dug on a hill looking down on the little valley they called home. The Irishman was laid to rest on a cold, cloudy day. Snow began to fall as they were throwing the last shovels of soil on their friend.

The remaining two Irishmen wrapped an arm around each other's back and raised a hand into the air.

"For the love of three sisters. Yes, for the love of three sisters." They then walked back to the cabin, tears running openly down their faces. For three friends were they. Yes, three friends, now two.

The blizzard raged outside all night long. The next day the sun was hidden behind dark clouds. By late afternoon, the snow started to fall again. The third day, the snow was at the bottom of the windows. It snowed early; usually the storms waited until after the New Year. It was just the first of December. No one was prepared for such a storm. Supplies still lay on shelves in town that would be purchased to survive weather like this later on.

The two friends sat out the storm and pondered their fate. Perhaps it was time to return to Ireland, they agreed. But yet much had to be done before such a thing could be. The mine could not just be left; someone else could come along and take possession of it. It was still yielding too much gold to just go off and abandon.

As the following night came upon them, the snow began to fall again. An hour or so after sundown their dog began to bark. They could hear what sounded like crying outside. Finally, one of them decided to go out and see what was making the noise. A few feet from the house, he could see a dark object bent over in a bundle. He walked up close and could see it was a young Indian child. He pulled on its clothing. As the head came into view, he could tell it was a young girl, probably eight or ten years old. She was almost frozen solid. He drug her into the cabin and put her close to the stove. They brought her warm tea and gently poured it into her mouth. When the Apache girl regained her strength, she made a leap to the front door. One of the Irishmen jumped up and prevented her escape. The second man went to the cupboard and brought back a piece of blue stone and gave it to the girl. She took it and pulled it to her. She looked at the man for a second, then turned her head quickly and looked down. They made her a mat on the floor by the fire and went to bed. Through the night they added wood to the fire to keep the girl warm. She slept soundly on her mat. The dog curled up by her feet.

The Irishmen had not forgotten their fallen friend lying outside in the frozen ground. Perhaps this child's father was the one who killed him. Still, looking into the eyes of this poor thing, it was hard to store grudges.

They named her "Wink" because she always laughed when they winked their eyes at her. She ate like a starved animal. It was easy to see the storm caught her people ill prepared as well.

The next day, the storm lifted and the sun began to shine. The two friends and Wink went outside to enjoy the warmth. Chores had to be done properly. The storm made it necessary to take some shortcuts. Stalls were in need of cleaning, feeding and watering to be done. At least it kept their minds off their fallen friend.

Wink pitched in and helped. She no longer feared them and it was satisfying to the two friends to have someone to care for. It made the time pass a little easier. In time, the snow melted and they could make it to the mine. One of the Irishmen decided he would go down and work a little. They no longer would make the progress they once did. Only one man could go down at a time. The other had to remain on top to work. It did not feel right, so they decided mining could wait.

Supplies needed to be purchased in case winter should make its early appearance again. The friends drew straws to see who would go into town. They would be hauling in some ore to be milled. The going would be slow. The other man would stay behind and work out some of the richer ore they had stockpiled. Wink would need looking after. And, besides, the weather had been good since the storm passed.

Wink was brushing one of the horses when the first Apache came riding up. The Irishman ran inside and grabbed his rifle. Soon several others joined the first Indian. They watched the place for awhile. Wink did not see them, the Irishman figured. He stayed in the shadows keeping his gun on the red men. They waved their arms around a little, making gestures to one another. Soon they rode away in the direction of the mine.

The partner was going to send word to the soldiers at Fort Grant and Ft. Bowie of the killing of the Irish miner by the Indians.

"Perhaps they would come out and teach them some manners," the remaining Irishman thought as the Indians rode away. He stayed close to home and kept the Winchester at hand in case he should need it.

Wink continued on with them, as if she preferred to live with them instead of her people.

After an absence of several days, the Irishman returned from town with some supplies. Cans of peaches were passed around. There was a new shirt to wear on Sundays, but no letters from home. Sadness gripped the Irishmen.

The Cavalry made good, and came and drove the last of the Indians out of Apache Canyon and took them to the agency at San Carlos. They persuaded the soldiers to leave Wink behind in their care. She became a daughter they never had.

The gold no longer could be put in one tree. It spilled over into other trees and Dutch ovens buried around the house. Still the Irishmen postponed their departure for Ireland. Several more years passed. The miners hit a pocket of gold of high quality with crystals and quartz laced nuggets of all shapes and sizes. Home would have to wait a little longer.

One day, just before noon, one of the men was in the shaft mucking out, when he struck a charge that hadn't gone off with the rest set for a blast. It exploded, powering a small rock, enough to embed itself into the side of the man's head. He died instantly. The Irishman on top knew something was wrong. No charges were set to go off this day. He ran to the house and got Wink, who was now big enough to work the hoist in an emergency. Down the shaft he was lowered. He hurried to where his friend was working. There, on the floor of the mine, he lay. Upon rolling him over he saw the rock in his head. Tears filled his eyes.

"Why? Why?" he cried out loud. He grabbed an ore cart and put his friend in it and rolled him to the hoist. Once on top, he could see more closely the damage that had been done.

The Irishman was laid to rest beside their other friend. Now, he alone was the surviving partner. He raised an arm in salute. "For the love of the three sisters were we. Yes, once three, now one."

The railroad had recently arrived in Maley, and they changed the name of the town to Willcox. The Irishman rode into the town and telegraphed of his friend's passing to the Irish Embassy in New York City and asked them to notify his family. He also told them to notify his own family of his planned return to Ireland.

They had bought a small bunch of cattle sometime ago; it prospered and they now had a sizeable herd. It would need attention in his absence. He hired a hand to care for the ranch and mine.

He began packing what he would be taking with him to Ireland. His two friends had a few possessions he would be returning to their families, as well as a share in the gold. A share would also be going to the three sisters. It was for their love that three lads had engaged in such a long quest. "Yes, it was only right," he thought as he filled buckskin bags with gold dust. Late into the night he worked. The gold was packed into well-made wooden trunks holding two hundred fifty pounds each of gold dust. With much difficulty they were loaded into the large wagon that had served him so well over the years.

The morning was filled with last minute directions to the new foreman. They mounted two of his best horses and rode the boundary of the ranch. The Irishman would be gone for quite a spell and he tried to do his best to make the new hand familiar with his spread. Mid afternoon found them back at the house. The Irishman changed his shirt and excused himself to the others and walked a short distance to the hillside where his friends were buried. There he knelt on one knee as if in prayer.

Wink looked up at the Irishman on the hill. She was saddened. The new foreman watched as she wiped at a tear with her handkerchief. She finally could not contain her self any longer; she walked out upon the porch.

"Father," she called loudly, "let us go!"

The Irishman rose up and walked slowly back to the house. He put an arm around his adopted daughter, and entered the kitchen. They ate some roast beef and potatoes, did some last minute packing and harnessed the wagon.

The Irishman went to his bed and sought out his six-gun hidden under it. He checked to see if it was in order. It was put it in a pocket sewn on the inside of his coat. He could get it quickly, if needed. Five hundred pounds of gold could buy a lot of trouble, he thought to himself.

He shook hands with the new man he had hired, jumped up on the wagon seat beside Wink, and gave the reins a shake.

"Get up, boys!" he called to the two horses.

Soon they were rounding a point of rock near the house. Beyond it lay the road to Willcox. They had to be at the station house by 6:00 o'clock in the evening.

Mixed emotion filled the Irishman as he left the mine and ranch behind. "Three sisters," he thought as the miles went by. "How many years has it been? A few gray hairs now invade a once black scalp. No, it couldn't be that long," he thought to himself. "Had it not been just yesterday he and his two friends left for California? Yes, kissed three redheaded lasses farewell? Aye, it had! Where had the days gone? Where did this gray hair come from?"

"Father, you are much to quiet!"

The words from Wink's mouth called him back from his current ramblings of thought. "It is true, my child, I have been."

The buildings of the settlement loomed ahead.

They pulled along the dock and unloaded the trunks containing the gold. They were entrusted to the railroad to deliver them safely to New York City.

They next took the wagon and horses to the livery stable. They would be returned to the ranch later by the new hand. All they could do now was wait.

The Irishman had drifted off to sleep, when the loud whistle of the steam locomotive filled his ears. It was still some distance away, but as it grew closer, he could feel the earth shake as it approached.

"Did you have a nice nap, father?" Wink asked.

"Yes, my child. My heart is heavy as we leave our home behind. Yet my home also awaits us in Ireland. You will not understand this for some time, but I now know what I stand to give up. In my youth in ignorance to this fact, I gave up my family and a red headed lass, one whom I should have stayed and married. Yet, I gave all this up to go traipsing around a land far from my home. Now I know what I am leaving behind as I take a voyage into the unknown. For so much time has passed, surely my parents have gone on, and my love married to another or perhaps herself returned to her maker. Still, this journey, though hard and long, must be made; for certain promises must be kept. Certain honors must be fulfilled. I'm sorry I ramble on so," the Irishman said, as he looked his daughter in the eye. "I will be alright," he laughed. "It's just hard to get underway; soon we will be in Ireland. I can't wait to show you off."

Wink smiled at her father, reached over and took his hand in hers.

The Irishman marveled at all the changes around him since leaving his desert home in Arizona; he had sped across this great land in comfort in the latest and fastest form of transportation.

He stood on the pier in New York about to embark on a voyage to his homeland on a large steamship, polished and painted beautifully. Such a different picture stood than what he saw as he left Ireland, in his youth, or perhaps his eyes had grown more accustomed to surveying his surroundings. "How could this day be better?" "Perhaps only if my two friends could have survived to share it with me. But, alas, dreams and nothing more fill this old man's head," he thought.

As he crossed the few steps it took to reach the deck of the ship, he extended his arm to steady Wink as she followed behind.

A young man in uniform approached them and offered to help them with the baggage. The Irishman smiled to himself as he watched this young man looking upon Wink's beauty. "This young Indian woman will turn the head of many an Irishman before this trip is over," he thought to himself.

Soon they were in their berth unpacking the things they would need on the voyage. The gold was stored deep in the bowels of the ship. The Irishman had checked the trunks upon arrival in New York to make certain the seals were undisturbed. "So far, all was well," he thought, as he pondered the gold.

Most likely the three beauties had long since married someone else. "Never mind," he thought. Promises were made and he would see that each would receive a portion of the gold retrieved from the ground by him and the sweat of his two friends. After all, they had made other promises to each other, which would not be broken by him. The two friends' share would go to their loves and a portion to his love. "This will be interesting," he thought as he daydreamed to himself.

Most of his evenings were filled with invitations from young men and families asking for Wink and himself to join them for dinner. "Wink has certainly become a hit," he thought. This bronze woman rescued by him and his partner from certain death had grown to be the most pleasing daughter a man could have. She always introduced him as 'her father' to everyone she met. This made the Irishman proud. She had returned culture in a life that had become hardened in a brutal land. Yet, this same land had given him her, the greatest gift he had ever received.

Thus, as he entered his cabin to rest on the final night of this voyage, his heart was glad. And the excitement that tomorrow might bring stirred him onward.

"Land! Land!" he heard as his eyes adjusted to the sunlight. He had come up on deck to get some fresh air.

"Yes, it is so!" he said under his breath, "It is my lovely homeland." A tear formed on the side of his eyes. He daubed at them, not wanting anyone to notice. "No need to worry," he thought. "Everyone is busy looking at the land coming into view."

He rushed below and opened his cabin door. "Wink!" he said excitedly. "Land is ahead; I saw it myself. You must hurry, my child, we will be docking soon."

With this, he turned and quickly exited his room and returned to the deck above.

The morning was filled with watching the cliffs of Ireland growing closer each passing hour. He did not remember when he saw the first house come into view. His mind, though trying, could not take in all the beauty at once. But there it was, a cottage on a hill slightly behind the cliffs. "Aye, Ireland it is!" he said to himself.

The ship was in Port when Wink came walking towards her father. A young man he had met earlier was escorting her. He was also carrying their bags.

"Father, I have our things! No need of going below again."

The Irishman smiled at his daughter.

The young man asked, "May I write?"

Wink, blushing slightly, said, "Please!"

He helped her cross the gangway to the land with the Irishman following along behind.

The Irishman first made arrangements with the captain for the gold to be transported to a bank for safe keeping. Next, a carriage was hired. Soon the cobblestone roads were left behind as they entered the countryside.

"Hold up, sir!" the Irishman called loudly to the driver.
The startled driver pulled to the side of the road.

The Irishman walked to the edge of a field circled in stacked rocks making a fence. Bending over, he picked up a handful of dirt. He raised it to his lips and kissed it. Then he rolled it over and over in his hand. He surveyed the landscape; then turning back to the carriage, he smiled at Wink. They were soon on their way again, the miles passing by quickly.

"There it is!" the Irishman said.

Wink looked the way he pointed.

"This is my father's home." They pulled up beside it. The Irishman quickly took the steps leading to the door. A knock brought several faces of young children peering out at him. He searched for someone he recognized, but to no avail. "I am here from America," he said.

He did not have time to say another thing before an old gray haired woman pushed through the children. The Irishman looked into her eyes, the same eyes he had looked into so often as he nursed at her breast as a child. "Momma!" he said.

They embraced for so long, a lifetime, for that is what had passed. You could not catch up on that easily.

"Momma, this is Wink, my step daughter. She is all the family I have in America. Wink, this is your grandmother."

The two embraced. It made the Irishman proud to see them accept each other so readily.

To see his mother once again made the long voyage worthwhile.

That night, a feast was held in his honor. Old friends filled his mother's house.

As of yet, he hadn't seen any of the three sisters. "Nary a one," he thought to himself. "Perhaps life has fallen hard upon them."

Then, as if in a dream, one came through the door. She was not the one who had filled his heart as a youth, but instead the one who had been close to the friend who the Apaches had arrowed above the mine. The same beautiful lines shaped her body as he remembered. She approached him. He extended his hands out to her and she took them in hers, then pulled him to her. After an embrace, he let her go a little and looked upon her face. I would do it again just to sample a moment like this." He pulled her to him again and once again held her tight, as if saying, "I lost you three once, I'll not lose you again."

The Irishman looked around the room and saw everyone looking at him. He blushed, and clapped his hands together. "My friends, everyone have fun!"

He still clung to one of her hands. He pulled her to one side of the room.

"How is it? How have you been? It's been so long!"

She smiled. "Which question shall I answer first?"

"Tell me everything," the Irishman encouraged.

"Where to begin?" she said. "First tell me how he died."

The Irishman looked down at the floor. "The Indians killed him. Might as well of died myself that day, that is how much it hurt. He never lost his love for you. We talked about you three girls the night I last saw him alive. He was totally committed to you."

A silence fell as the two gave thought to the fallen friend.

The Irishman's insides begged for information about the other two sisters, especially the one he loved so much. This time, he could tell something-weighed heavy on her mind.

She started out softly: "I regret to be the one to inform you." She stumbled with the words. "They are both married. Happily, I assure you, but knowing how you must feel, I regret being the one to bear this news."

The Irishman was crushed. He knew, in coming, it was a small chance she would still be available, yet a small chance avails hope. Now, hope lay extinguished at his feet, for words of truth had just put it there.

It was then he noticed a hand rubbing through the hair on the back of his neck. It was the hand of this redheaded lass, one of the trio, he and his two friends had dreamed about for so many years.

"And what about you?" he asked then paused.

"What do you mean?" she questioned.

"Are you married as well?"

"No!" she said. "I was the romantic fool who waited for a man to return to me one day, from his quest for gold, to claim my hand and pay my father handsomely for it." Now it was she, who emotion held so tightly.

The Irishman paused for a moment, then took her by the hand. He held it to his lips and kissed it gently. "I will be that man if you will let me."

She withdrew her hand for a moment, then extended it back to him. "I guess it would only be right," she said as she smiled.

The Irishman once again embraced her. He said; "We have a lot of catching up to do. Will you return with me to America?"

"If you want me to," she said.

"So many years had led up to this night; so many hardships, so much loss. Yet so much happiness it now spawns," the Irishman thought.

They were married the next day. No more precious days would be lost to chance, they both agreed. This day forward they would take charge of their lives, their love.

"Paris would be a proper place for a honeymoon," the Irishman said to his new wife.

"My man, do we have this kind of money?" she asked.

"This much and more!" the Irishman said proudly. "We did find gold, you know. I brought some back to you and your two sisters since you were all part of this; they would have wanted it this way, as well as myself. Let's give it to them and then be off to Paris."

The sisters were surprised to see the bags of gold stacked on the table.

The Irishman told of the "Three Sisters' Mine" in Arizona, how it had yielded gold after much sacrifice by all. "It is right you have it as a token of our friendship."

Arm in arm, the Irishman and his wife left the room.

The Irishman made arrangements for Wink to stay with his family in Ireland while he and his new bride went to Paris. They rented a Villa there for a month. The woman bought furnishings for a home in Arizona she had only heard about from her husband. Undeterred, she was determined to make a home of refinement of it. The Irishman's only purchase was to find a stone carver who could make proper head stones for his two friends. He figured they should share in some way from this wealth.

"These will be the two fanciest head stones in Arizona!" he said proudly to his wife when they saw them.

The month ended and once again the Irishman found himself boarding a ship headed for Ireland. He made his way back to his mother's home. There he entertained a constant troupe of visitors and well wishers. People from his youth spoke as it were only yesterday they met last. Yet, a lifetime for some had transpired. The balance of the gold he had brought with him to give to the family of his two friends was divided. It made him happy to see hope once again fill the faces of those who had mourned for the loss of his two friends.

Late one night he grew restless. He asked if his wife would like to join him at the local pub for a glass of ale.

"A woman should not enter a place of that nature. But if you wish, I will accompany you there," she said.

"You are right. I have forgotten some of our local customs," the Irishman said.

He secured a horse from a family member and rode by himself to the pub he had been to so many times in his youth.

"This place hasn't changed much," the Irishman said as the barkeep wiped the bar in front of him.

"You new in town?" the man asked.

"No sir, not new; it's been awhile, however. An old man with one eye worked here the last time I was here abouts."

"That would be my father," the man said.

"He was a wise man," the Irishman said. "Wish I would have listened to him. "Would you please set up three glasses of your best Irish whisky?"

The bar keep looked puzzled since he was alone. The silence remained unbroken as the younger man did as he was requested. With the three glasses poured, the Irishman said to the man, "Excuse me, please," and turned and faced the doorway. Raising one of the glasses he said, "For the love of three sisters, yes, the love of three sisters." He paid the barkeep and walked towards the door.

The ride home was short. He would have preferred it be longer. That would have given him more time to sort out the many thoughts in his mind. He came to the conclusion that his trip must soon be over. He had accomplished all he sought to do. It was time to put the past behind him. His mother would be well cared for with the gold dust he had given her. Already his brothers were adding more rooms on her home. One of them would be on hand at all times to care for her. "Yes, he must be getting home," he thought. It was at this moment he knew for sure that home was not here any longer. The land of the Apache in Arizona was his home.

"Wink, let's go home!" the Irishman said to his daughter as he entered her sleeping quarters.

"So soon, father?" she asked. He couldn't help but see the disappointed look upon her features.

"What is it, my child? Have you something holding you to this place?" She turned away not wanting her hurt to show on her face.

"Have you met someone while I was in Paris?" he asked.

She was shocked at how soon he had come to that conclusion. "A young man calls on me father. He makes my insides feel all warm when I'm with him."

The Irishman remained quiet.

The girl volunteered. "It is your wife's, my stepmother's, nephew."

"And who might this young man's mother be?" the Irishman queried.

"His mother is the one you loved as a young man."

"At least you have good taste, my child. What will you do about him?" he asked.

"He has asked me to marry him, and I accepted." The Irishman was shocked to say the least. He left the room to seek counsel with his wife.

"Love is not a thing to interfere with," she said. "Let our lives be a lesson to this. I pray you let the child marry with your blessing, even as my father should have done in our youth."

"You are as wise as you are beautiful," he said as he kissed her on the forehead.

The wedding was the most talked about thing in the town's recent history. The two were married and gold from the "Three Sisters' Mine" flowed freely that day. The best of everything was on hand for the occasion. The Irishman kissed the new bride extra long, for it was also to be goodbye since he would be on his way back to Arizona before they returned from their honeymoon.

The Irishman sat on the deck of the ship, napping. He felt the hand of his wife rest upon his shoulder. Waking up slightly, he reached to pull her down to a chair beside him.

"Funny thing," he said. "Love has a way of its own. I desired your sister, yet love gave me you. It gave my love's son to my stepdaughter, thus passing love to another generation. Yet here now in your arms, I confess, love is wiser than I."

She gripped his hand tightly to show her approval with his words. Soon the Irishman was once again napping.

The train's whistle blew loudly as it approached the little town of Willcox, Arizona. The Irishman could see the foreman from his ranch through the car's window. He gave him a wave and a smile as the train drew to a stop. Hellos were exchanged. News was quickly shared. The Irishman was impatient to get underway. They made arrangements to have their belongings brought to the ranch by some local teamsters.

The town grew faint in the background as the Irishman shared insight with his wife on names of mountains and local plants. The trip to the ranch seemed to pass quickly. They rounded a ledge of rocks and the house came into view.

"This is your new home, my love. For a life time I dreamed of sharing this with an Irish Rose, Yea, lass, you don't disappoint me none."

They came to a stop by a hitching rail. The Irishman carried his wife through the front door and planted her on the floor.

"It's beautiful!" was all she said.

The next few days were spent exploring the far reaches of the ranch. The Irishman taught her to throw a rope in their spare time. Happiest in each other's arms, the nights passed quickly.

"How do you expect me to learn to catch one of those critters?" she asked, as she threw the lasso and missed.

"I don't," he said with a smile. "You caught me and that was all you need to catch."

"We must still make a living on this land," she replied.

"We have the cattle, horses and the mine. Most of all we have each other. The rest will take care of itself," the Irishman assured her.

The moon rose full, as it cleared the mountains to the east; it was as if it were daylight once more.

"Let's go for a walk," the man said as he reached for his lady's hand.

Outside, a sweet smell filled the air. A night blooming cirrus cactus blossomed. Its' one night of glory was shared with the two lovers.

"Over here!" he said as he pulled the woman along the stone lined creek bottom. An oak tree growing there was his destination. He reached inside a hole unobserved by her before his hand entered it. He pulled out a leather bag and gave it to her.

"Gold!" he said as he smiled. He returned his hand with another, then another.

"Wait a minute, these are heavy!" she said laughing as she threw one back to him. "How much of this stuff is there?"

"See that tree over there? And those two there... And those. They are all full of gold. Also, some Dutch ovens and fruit jars are buried over there to the east. We will hire cow hands to rope the cattle," the Irishman said as they returned to the house.

"For the love of three sisters!" he said as he drew the woman close to him. His hand quickly found the back of her head. He pulled the comb from her hair, allowing it to fall freely down her back. He grabbed a coil of hair and used it to pull her closer to him. Her hair looked like gold as the flickers of lantern light played upon it.

He said quietly to himself: "Now the love of one sister," as his lips found hers.

STOLEN HORSES
Chapter 11

For two days, the Indian horseman rode on oblivious to the fact that he was bent on accomplishing a task that was near impossible. His horse was tiring quickly and his body cried loudly for rest. Yet he pressed on, his honor bound him to a code of ethics understood by few, except his people, a native group accustomed to the hardships of the arid Southwest. If he should fail, death awaited him in the hands of those he pursued. He would also fail if he did not retrieve the band of horses that were stolen from his people two days before.

He had ridden over to the soldiers' Fort at White River, Arizona Territory. It was supposed to be an uneventful buying of supplies. He had stayed one day longer than he had planned. A cousin of his had given birth to a boy child. He lingered on to pay his respect. The agency had gathered most of his people from their former lands and brought them to live around the Fort. It was here that he witnessed the continuing of the cycle of life.

As he approached his rancheria, he could see the dust of many horses on the horizon. Upon entering the compound, it was obvious they were his horses. He reined up by his home. His family was standing in the tree line watching, not knowing if the approaching rider was he or one of the intruders returning. A cry was answered, and soon all his family members were gathered around him exchanging words, explaining what had happened. It seems they were surprised at daybreak by a band of Mexicans, who promptly broke through the brush corral and drove the horses down the Salt River towards the west.

Since all the horses but the one he was riding was stolen, he alone would give chase. First, his mount was fed and watered, then he gave a farewell wave and rode off. He could not go far before dark, but he could not let them lengthen the distance between him and them. Many lives depended on the horses.

It's hard to ride in the rough broken and brush choked land of central Arizona at night. The rustlers, as well as himself, must seek rest and wait for the light of day to proceed. The winds picked up in the night and began to push a storm front through the land of the Apache. Morning found a red haze in the mountains, as if mimicking a sunset. For a moment the Indian surveyed the beauty around him. Then reality gripped him and he gathered his horse and was on his way. Soon the rain spirits would appear, the Indian thought, as he hurried onward. He must catch up to the thieves before the storm came and washed away the tracks of the fleeing horses. As the day progressed, he thought it best to climb further up the steps above the river and see if he could spot those he pursued. Before he reached the top, the rains began. Violent lightning bolts screamed across the sky. The thunder voices cried loudly to announce their arrival. The Indian sought shelter in a nearby overhang of rock. It was not deep, but it allowed him and his horse enough room to get in away from the rain. Quietly the Indian sat in deep thought, marveling how the earth changes so suddenly. It was while thus in thought; a bolt of lightning struck a dead cedar tree in the narrow draw below him. Not once, but three times, the tree felt the thrust of the mighty power of the gods. The tree burst into flames as the rain poured down around it. The Indian now focused in new awe. For him, this was medicine. The gods were telling him not to proceed any further at this time. A gate now stood ablaze between him and the thieves. The Indian watched as the tree began to break apart, and branches fell to the wet ground. He abruptly stood up and walked over to his horse and turned him loose to graze. This night would come and pass on this very spot. He rested easy, as he no longer felt the urgency to chase onward.

Morning was still to be when shots brought him back from slumber. He rose up and strained his ears towards the direction the shots came from. A pause, then a few more shots; they could not be very far away. The Indian sprang towards his horse just as the burning tree once again surfaced in his memory. He paused, then sat on a rock overlooking the valley below. Daylight would soon be at hand. He would wait, then proceed cautiously onward.

When the shadows began to flee the rising sun, he made his way back down to the river bottom. He hadn't gone far when he saw the first of the dead ones. Then more lay on the ground ahead, the same amount as the fingers on one hand. All he recognized as kinsman from the village of Cibicue.

Anger once again flowed through his mind. He shook for a moment in rage. How dare these Mexicans steal his horses and now kill innocent people unaware of the danger lurking in their path. He carefully carried the dead men to a crevice in the rock cliffs close by. He lowered them into one and piled rocks on the top of them. This would keep the animals from doing further damage. As he rode on, he thought once again about the former night when the gods placed a fiery gate between him and certain death. Had he continued he would be the same as the dead men he had just found.

This was not the first time he had been preserved by a greater power. Once before, in his youth, his life had been spared. He had journeyed far from his father's camp. His quest was to find medicine that would reveal his purpose for being here upon Mother Earth. After much fasting and prayer, he had accomplished nothing. Try as he might, he could not summons the spirits to attend to his desire. So the vigil continued many days. Pangs of hunger stung his belly; his mind grew faint. Death was at hand. Water was scant and he was too weak to go and retrieve more. On the final morning, the Great Spirit in the form of a crow landed on his belly as he lay dying. It bounced up and down summonsing his attention. He tried to shoo it away so as to die in peace. The crow would only hop up an arm's distance and drop back down on him, scolding him loudly. It was then that a vision was played before his eyes. If he lost focus, the bird would pinch him soundly with its beak. After what seemed a lifetime, the bird flew to a near by rats' nest under a cedar tree. There he scratched out many pinion nuts the rats had hidden carefully for winter. After seeing the crow's find, the Indian weakly crawled over to the cache of nuts and ate his fill. Thus sustained, his strength returned. He made his way back to his father's home. Years had passed since that day, yet now once again he had been spared.

Miles began to lengthen between him and his family. Onward he rode, stopping only enough to rest his horse and stretch his aching muscles. He must somehow gain the upper hand.

His mind once again drifted to his youth. The message the Great Spirit revealed to him was cloudy in places. He had devoted his life to finding out what it was He wanted him to do. He had followed in the teachings of his grandfather. It was he who took him by the hand and led him into manhood after his father was killed at Apache Pass.

The Old One sees no more with his eyes. Clouds cover them and keep him in darkness, yet he sees more than ever. The Old One looks with his spirit. Yes, he should be more like the ancient one, the rider thought, as he worked his way through a steep canyon leading up from the river.

The thieves were finally heading up a narrow canyon to the mesa tops. Opportunity might present itself to suprise them. He edged his horse onward with a small slap to his rump. The tracks were once again easy to follow. The rains came early in the day and did not last long. His stallion grew impatient to catch up to the band of mares and colts. He did not need much encouraging. The Indian knew he was close by the horse's behavior.

The Indian had caught this horse several winters ago. It came down from the high country to winter on the plains by Black River. The horse was swift as an eagle in flight as he ran across the rolling hills. He knew he must have this animal. Did he not move out in the wilds with him until it was so? The Old One laughed when he said what he was going to do. But later, he heard him bragging to the old men how his grandson was going after the stallion. Yes, he knew the horse would be his. It wasn't until the next winter the rider and horse came back into the camp of his grandfather. He had followed the horse back to the mountains that summer. It was there he was captured and broken to ride. Great fun that was, he reminisced. Everyone gathered around as he rode in that day. The horse was heavily muscled and proud; he sat up tall on the back of this stallion. Now, many winters later, he was still sitting tall on the same animal. Many mares had been covered by it and his herd increased in size. The blood of this fine horse now flowed in most of them, except they were now in the hands of the Mexicans. Soon he would right this situation.

The clouds once again gathered for an evening shower. The rider sought shelter under a cedar tree. Deer and elk had bedded there recently. It would now serve him as well. His horse was tied, for fear he might rush to the horses he trailed.

A leather bag was lying on his lap as he sharpened his knives. He wore two, one on each hip, razor sharp. One, then the other, was returned to its sheath. Next he took out red ochre and white kaolin and painted his face. A piece of black obsidian was removed from the bag; he struck it, causing a small chip to break away. He used it to carefully cut a small incision above each breast causing blood to ooze down the front of him. This would be the only blood he lost this day. The Great Spirit had assured him this. He stood up as the rain had stopped. A bullet was chambered in his rifle; a leather strap allowed it to hang down his back. A quick spin and it was in his hand doing its deadly work if it need be.

The sun was just a sliver as he led the stallion to the trail they had been following. He had previously taken a short cord from the leather bag. It was tied around the horses' neck and then to a stout branch of a small oak tree. This accomplished; the Indian proceeded ahead on foot. Silent as the fox, he moved into the night. The moon was well into flight across the dark sky when he smelled the horses. Then a faint noise was heard. As he drew closer, he could see the animals scattered about grazing. The men were in the shadows out of view, so he worked his way closer. He could hear the sound of metal striking rocks; the Mexicans horses were shod while his was not. It was only a matter of time and they would come to him. Carefully he crawled closer to the horses. Ahead lay a grove of cedar trees. He would hide in them until the thieves appeared.

Once the Indian's eyes became accustomed to the darkness inside the grove of trees, he continued on. He was almost across it when he came upon what he thought was one of the Mexicans sleeping. He drew his knife and crawled silently. Grabbing the unsuspecting person from behind, he felt the softness of a woman; he paused for a second as she told him to "get away, you dog." Putting his hand over her mouth, he prevented any further sound. He rolled her over so he could see her and motioned for her to be silent. The woman's eyes betrayed her fear, but no further sound escaped her lips. The Indian saw she was one of his people. He spoke to her 'in sign' and told her he had come to reclaim his horses and that she would be safe with him. Thus assured, she found new strength to help him seek revenge on her captives. He cut the leather bands they had tied her with. She rubbed vigorously to restore circulation to her hands.

As they sat in the shadows looking at each other, the sounds of approaching hooves drew his attention. The Indian lay flat on the ground; he could see bedrolls and tack in the clearing beyond him. This is when the Mexican rider appeared. The Indian watched the woman to see if her eyes showed any sign of betrayal; there was none. He then turned to size up the Mexican. He was a large man, well built. A pistol hung on his hip and a large round hat was on his head. He wore tall-heeled boots; both would be to his disadvantage on the rough malapai ground they were on. The Mexican threw back a blanket and exposed some wood, then proceeded to add some to the fire. The Indian told the woman to call out to the Mexican. He swore at her and kept on building the fire. Minutes passed. Suddenly the Mexican walked towards the woman. As he stood before her, he asked her what she wanted. She said she was hungry. The Indian stood behind him and plunged his knife into the Mexican's liver and pulled up. The Mexican crumpled in a pile on the ground, dead. The woman stood up beside the Indian and wrapped her arms around him. She needed assurance from him, he, in turn, put his arm around her and held her tight. He drug the body of the Mexican back into the trees. He kicked dirt and leaves over the blood. They would now wait for another rider to show.

It wasn't long before they heard once again the sound of an approaching rider, then another. The Indian dropped to one knee and cocked his rifle. Eyes straining into the darkness. Finally, two riders appeared next to the dancing fire. Each tied his horse to the same bush as their dead friend had done. They talked loudly to each other as they stood by the fire. As one bent over to retrieve a stick of wood, the Indian placed a bullet at the base of his neck. The Mexican rolled over backwards into the bed of coals. Before the sound of the first shot had ended, a second report issued so fast they blended as one; the second Mexican lay dying on top of the one in the fire pit.

The roar of the gun sounded as thunder in the narrow canyon. The horses raised their heads, sniffed the air, and bottled back down the trail the way they came. The Indian fired more shots into the side of the cliffs to encourage them onward. He knew the horses would run to the stallion waiting where he had tied him. The stallion would pull free and lead them back to the rancheria.

He remained low to the earth in the shadows, watching to see if any more Mexicans were unaccounted for. He did not know if he should trust the Indian woman with his life or not. He realized that if he asked her how many had held her captive, he would be bound to believe her. He wanted her to volunteer such information of her own free will. Then he could ponder it in his mind and try to figure out where they stood. She did not move to expose herself to the darkness, so he remained likewise.

The two Mexicans' clothes burned and lit up the camp. The smell of burning flesh filled the air. The Indian strained his ears for the slightest sound. Finally it came. A twig snapped behind him. He rolled over just as the final Mexican lunged at him with his knife held high. The Mexican buried his knife in the spot the Indian had been laying. In a heartbeat the Mexican tried to roll over to face the Indian, but was wedged against a cedar tree and could not bring himself into a position of defense. The Indian pressed his own knife into the Mexican, at the same time pulling his broad hat over his eyes with his other hand.

The Indian woman stood up and once again put her arms around her rescuer. Tears snuck out the corner of her eyes. She turned her head so he could not see. But the Indian felt the moist drops run down his arm.

The Indian did not wish to sleep in this place of death. He looked around and gathered a few things he would take back to his people. He saved a couple of pistols and knives. One bag was so heavy it took two hands to lift it. He opened it and peered inside; sacks of dust and large nuggets filled the bag. The yellow glow shone as the fire danced on it. "Yellow metal," was all he said. He carried it over and put it on the third horse. He then led a horse over to the woman. He handed her the rein. With one jump, he was on the remaining horse and riding away. The woman followed along. Once again, on the banks of the Salt River, they paused for the night. The Indian hobbled the horses since they were not accustomed to him. He made a bed, the best he could for the woman. Then he walked to the river and jumped in. He swam a long distance, rolled over and returned. He then sat in the sand, water running over his legs. The moistened blood now streaked down his belly. He took his hand and rubbed it around. Finally, he jumped back in the deep water and rinsed off. He stood up shivering in the night breeze. He walked over and collapsed on the ground close to the woman.

The sun's brightness woke up the slumbering Indians. He looked around for a moment to get his bearings. He had slept well this night and felt refreshed. It had been a difficult trip so far. But he hoped the difficult part was over.

He grabbed his rifle and headed down the river bottom. He had hardly left when the woman heard the report of the rifle. She marveled at this man's good fortune. A short distance from camp she found him bent over a deer. Blood was running from his lips as he chewed a piece of the deer's liver. He rose up enough to offer her a piece, then bent back over to finish his task. She, too, chewed the piece of meat like the man. They dragged the deer back to camp and built a fire to roast part of it. Soon they were laughing and having fun as they ate their fill. The rest of the flesh was hung on the branches of a nearby tree to dry.

The woman turned around and walked toward the river without speaking a word. The Indian continued fussing with the meat strips he was placing out to dry. She did not return for what seemed a long time, so he followed her tracks toward the river. Her back was to him as she bent over, combing at her hair. She was wet and the moisture glistened off her bronze back and buttocks. He stopped and stepped back into the shadows, pausing briefly to soak in her beauty. Then he turned and walked another way back to camp. He did not want her to know he had been searching for her.

He was taking stock of the Mexicans' possessions when she returned to camp. She, once again, had tears in her eyes. She looked away, but he could not help but notice. He smiled at her, trying to make her feel better. She returned his smile and the tears vanished.

They saddled the horses and rode towards home. The Indian stopped by a small cave in a cliff at the river's edge. He cut a green stick and made a point on it. Then he went in the cave and dug a hole against the back wall. In it, he placed the bag of gold. Layers of rocks were laid on the top of it, then the dirt was returned to the hole. No trace of digging could be seen. He then threw the stick in the river and rode back to camp. They built a simple shelter in case the rain returned. The afternoon was spent in resting.

The Indian spoke first when he saw the woman had awakened. "I marvel at your beauty," he said softly.

She did not return his gaze, but instead looked at the ground.

"Are you afraid of me?" he asked.

She still remained quiet.

"Do you have children, perhaps a husband as well?" he asked.

She shook her head no to this question, but still maintained her gaze to the ground.

"Let's go for a walk," he said, as he offered her his hand.

She looked up and took his hand and smiled at him.

They walked down the river's edge, feet in the water. It was not long before they were playing like children, splashing and throwing water at each other. As the sun sank behind the cliffs above, they made their way back to camp and started a fire to cook an evening meal. Deer meat and wild onion stew was soon simmering on the fire.

After the meal was eaten, they sat around looking into the dancing flames. After a silence, the Indian asked her how she came to be a prisoner of the Mexicans.

"They captured me as I carried water home at the Sky Pueblo, Acoma. They rode off with me before anyone knew of my predicament. They were taking me to Mexico to be sold as a slave in the silver mines. They used my body to do as they saw fit." With this, she began to weep again.

He asked no further questions. He sat silently feeling good that he had strength to prevail over the four Mexicans for they deserved to die. He picked up a small stick and began to poke at the fire. They slept this night speaking no further.

The Indian knew he should return to his people, yet something made him want to remain here with this woman, who he had rescued from the Mexicans. A new feeling, unfamiliar to him, awakened inside and threatened to consume him. This woman was from a distant land, a land he had never been to. A Sky Pueblo, she called it. A mystery hung over her; a mystery overtook him as well.

A new day came to the land of the Apache. The Indian woke first but remained quiet looking into the face of the woman. He had done so since day break. He didn't want her to stir and break the spell. Something about this woman pulled feelings from inside of him, ones that he had never experienced before. Just as these thoughts passed through his mind, her eyes opened. He smiled at her.

"What are you looking at?" she asked.

"Nothing," the Indian replied.

"I saw you looking at me," she said with a smile. "Do you like what you see?"

"Yes!" the Indian replied.

She turned her head quickly and looked away.

Quietness engulfed them. The Indian tried several times to get her to speak some more, but she held her tongue. He finally grabbed her hand and said, "Let's go to the river."

She rose up and smiled. They ran down the bank to a deep pool. They jumped in and swam around, chasing each other. After awhile, the Indian walked out in the shallow water. He removed his clothes and began to pound them with a rock to clean them. Soon the woman joined him and did the same. The man smiled approvingly as he looked at the naked woman. They hung their clothes in a small tree and retreated back in the water. They once again swam and chased each other around. During a moment of silence, he swam over and put his arm around the woman. She turned to face him. He drew her close and kissed her. Tears once again formed in the corners of her eyes. She pulled away from the man and ran towards camp. He gathered the clothes from the branches and followed after the woman. He found her on her bedding, crying. He approached her and lay down beside her. He twisted her hair around his finger. "What is the matter? Do you not approve of me?"

She sobbed louder, but managed to speak. "They hurt me, they hurt me! Can you be happy with a woman such as I? Or do you desire me only for a moment's pleasure as they?" She managed to control her sobs, but she still spoke very softly.

"I offer sincere feelings," he replied.

"Even though they sowed their seed in me? And at this time I might be with their child? Does this make a difference to a great warrior as yourself?"

"It is I who killed the ones who did this to you. It is I who gained great satisfaction in doing so. Now let us put this painful thing behind us and let love take its natural course."

A smile appeared on her lips as he drew her to him. As he held her close, he asked if she would be his wife. She, in turn, asked if he would be a husband to her. They agreed that it must be good.

The Indian spent the afternoon building a sweat lodge to purify both of them. They heated rocks and carried them into the lodge. After sweating profusely, they jumped into the river. After several times of repeating this, the sun disappeared behind the cliffs above.

He pulled the woman to him and said, "I give myself to you."

She hugged him and said, "I am your wife. Be good to me, my husband."

The man and woman repeated a night played over and over again down the ages, a night of shared love. A night of joy on the bank of a river that had been moving water to the ocean for equally as long.

As the first rays of light spilled over the cliffs upon the faces of the two below, the woman plucked a grass straw and began to tickle the man on the nose. He opened one eye, saw what she was doing and began to laugh.

He grabbed her and once again pulled her to himself. "The night was too short!" he said, as he buried his head in her breasts.

Later in the day they gathered the gear and rounded up the stock. They rode towards home. In the afternoon, they met a group of relatives riding on the returned horses. The front rider was leading the horse the Old One was on. The Indian rode up to him.

"Grandfather, I have a wife!"

"I know!" the old man said smiling.

"How do you know?" the Indian asked him. "I saw her, I was with you at the river, nice buttocks!" he added.

"I should of known." the Indian said softy. "My wife, this is Quintero, my Grandfather."

THE SANDAL
Chapter 12

When they buried grandfather, the grandson took the name of Quintero as his own, thereby keeping the name alive, and its strong medicine. Grandfather would approve of it, he thought.

Quintero grew restless; the earth had not yet received rain since his grandfather's passing.

"Let us leave this place for awhile and journey to the land of my people, the land of my grandfather's youth. Perhaps we will find rain there. It would help wash our sorrow away, my wife."

"The seasons have came and gone one time since our marriage. I wish to honor this with blue stone for you to wear. I will make beads of it to enhance your beauty. There is a place in that land where they dig it from the earth. Three Irishmen search for yellow metal."

"Why had not your grandfather put a stop to it, my husband?" the woman asked.

"It is true, they would not of been able to continue digging as they have, but for the blue stone. Grandfather and the Chiefs of his people thought it must be a sign to let them be. Even yet, one of his cousins attacked and killed one of the men. It is odd, my wife; this same cousin's child sought refuge with the two remaining men after her father was killed in Mexico. They raised her as their own. Strong medicine comes from this place where they dig sacred stone."

The next morning they were well on their way. Many miles had passed since they left their Rancheria on the Salt River. The heat of the day found them under some large oak trees to gain shade. The horses were grazing nearby.

At first, it was only the slightest breeze. Then the air currents grew stronger. A dust devil sought grass and dirt and raised it into the sky.

"The Wind Spirits grow restless," Quintero said to his wife. "Soon it will rain. Let us seek shelter in the rocks ahead," he told her as he hurried towards the grazing animals.

He had hardly caught them when they heard the first deep rumble of thunder in the canyon bottoms below them. Then it grew louder as it came closer. Smiles filled the faces of husband and wife as they rode hard on swift horses towards the cliffs above them. The trail was steep, but they knew they could make it there before the rain started, so they hurried onward. The sky darkened as the rains came. Sheets of water poured down hiding the ridges across the canyon before them.

Quintero started a small fire from sticks he found in the back of the cave. Pack rats had built a large nest there so small pieces of wood were plentiful. After the fire burned for awhile, Quintero removed his clothes and went out into the rain. He laughed loudly, and encouraged his wife to do the same. She retrieved some yucca root from her bags and dropped her clothes to the ground beside his. The rain was cool to the two travelers, but it was what they sought. Both were happy and gave thanks for their good fortune. They scrubbed each other with soap and washed their hair. They sought shelter by the fire as the cold bit them.

Quintero hoped most of all the rain would also wash away the sorrow of losing the Old One. They decided this day to put grief away. Had not the earth renewed itself? Would it not do them as well to do the same? Quintero felt good about these thoughts. He would make a shrine for the Old One in his homeland. He would also make fetishes of the blue stone and leave them there. There he would leave some of his possessions he saved for this purpose. Then it would be done. The Old One could rest in the land of the dead.

Quintero was deep in thought as he watched the sun once again pass through the clouds. It hung low on the horizon and would soon be gone.

"Quintero rested well this day," his wife said as she sat down beside him. She handed him some dried meat. He began to chew it as they watched the sunset fade.

The fire died down for lack of attention. Quintero rose up and walked to the back of the rock ledge. There he found more sticks to add to the fire. He bent over and saw a small woven sandal of a child.

"A former guest here must have lost it," he thought, as he picked it up and carried it back by the fire. It was made of yucca fiber, tightly woven and of good quality. It was well worn, revealing, most likely it was discarded from wear. He handed it to the woman. She took it and examined it closely. She smiled at him.

"Perhaps this is an omen," she said.

Quintero smiled back at her and said, "Perhaps."

The woman sat by the fire and turned the sandal over many times observing it from all angles, as if to not miss anything. She was sensing its spirit, trying to know its former owner, or perhaps the message it brought to them. Quintero lay back in silence as he watched her.

At first light, the two travelers were once again astride their horses working there way south. They crossed over the divide and were now heading into the great valley below. It would lead them, after many more miles, into the next valley containing Metate Mound.

"This would be their first destination," Quintero thought as they rode on. He had been there many times with his grandfather. This would be the first with the woman he loved.

Once again, the afternoon brought rain. This time they made a shelter of juniper branches. Quintero marveled at how quickly the woman was able to construct it. They sat inside watching the rain fall to the earth. The woman brought the yucca sandal from a bag and once again examined it. Quintero held his silence.

After some time had passed, the woman turned to him and spoke softly, "Perhaps my husband will form a child in me on this trip!"

Quintero looked at his wife; she was ever full of surprises. That is what he liked most about her. "So open, so loving," he thought. He was lucky to have her. He knew the Great Spirit had put them together. Yet many seasons had come and gone and still no child had been conceived. He would greatly like to grant her wish. All he could say to her though was; "Perhaps." This brought a smile to her face. She stood up and let her clothing fall to the ground. "So direct!" Quintero thought as he watched her undress. It had the effect she desired. Afterwards, contented, they lay in each other's arms in the cedar wikiup as the rain pounded the earth outside. The infant sandal lay at the doorway, inviting a baby spirit to enter in.

Quintero now wondered if his trip to Metate Mound was of utmost importance. Perhaps they were here instead to partake of this moment he had just shared in the arms of his wife.

His wife's movements brought Quintero back to the present. His thoughts returned to her. Pangs of hunger shot through his stomach. It was only then that he realized he had not eaten since the night before.

"I am hungry!" Quintero said.

"Is not my love enough to satisfy your appetite, my husband?"

"Yes, you do that very well, my love, but man must eat to keep up his strength. For I work hard trying to please you as well."

"Is love hard then, my husband?"

"No, it is easy. It is hard not to love someone, especially you," he said.

She smiled as she went to their belongings and retrieved food for them to eat.

Quintero smiled as he watched the woman move around, still disrobed, it pleased him. He also knew this woman was not going to give up easily. She was determined he was going to grant her wishes.

She once again bent over and picked up the yucca sandal in the doorway. She put it in her bag lying on the ground. After seeing to its safety, she sat next to her husband and began to rub his heavily muscled back.

Darkness caught them ill prepared, between the rain and his wife's urgent needs. Quintero had not gathered any firewood. The darkness drove them into their shelter, where love once again held them. Now the woman lay in deep sleep. He watched the stars through the opening of his shelter, as he lay contemplating what to do. The rain is what he sought. Now it made travelling difficult. "The heat that brings it, boils up from the desert below," he thought.

"Metate Mound will wait until the heat subsides." Now he decided to return to his Rancheria, enjoy the rain and watch the stalks of corn he planted grow.

Perhaps he would soon see sign of his wife's belly growing as well. These thoughts made it easy for Quintero to rest. He rolled over and put his arm around his wife as she lay beside him sleeping.

QUINTERO BATTLES THE DARK RIDERS
Chapter 13

Quintero was happy his wife had grown to know his grandfather before he returned to the land of the Spirits. This man who had such an influence on his life had also helped her heal after her ordeal with her captives. The satisfaction of killing these men fell on him alone, but it was his grandfather who taught him how to help her regain her former self, thereby remaining one person and not living another life in her dreams. It was these dreams that awoke him many times in the night as she battled imaginary attackers. He would hold her close until she could once again find peace. It was his grandfather's strong medicine that was able to drive these demons from the dream world away. The same medicine he now possessed, had been passed down to him by the Old One. His wife was now whole, one person, whose beauty was not only upon her skin, but inside her as well. Here is how it happened:

Hidden in the rocks, looking down on the desert, the lone Indian strained his senses trying to discover who was firing the shots far below him. The unmistakable crack of a rifle reached his ears for the second time. Then, many more followed, finally silence. He watched and listened without any sign where they came from. Then he caught the sight of a riderless horse. As it drew closer to him, he saw an arrow sticking up from the swells in its saddle.

"Arrows make no noise," he said under his breath.

The horse continued on in the distance until it was no longer visible.

Only silence remained, as he once again surveyed the desert below. The only movement he saw was a red tail hawk in flight, circling, looking for prey. The Indian, like the hawk watched, waiting for something to move, thereby revealing itself.

A covey of quail scratched around a prickly pear cactus for seeds left behind as others ate of its succulent fruit. A rooster sounded warning as the hawk drew closer. A screech from the hawk caught his attention as it rode an updraft from the canyon floor. It climbed higher and higher into the sky as the Indian returned his attention to watching below him. Still there was no sign of movement from the direction where he heard the shots.

He had left his home on the Salt River, Arizona Territory many days ago. He had stayed at Metate Mound longer than he should have. The spirit of his people was strong there. He had meditated long, trying to seek counsel with the Great Spirit. His wife, now great with child, remained at his Rancheria. Weakness kept her unable to leave her bed but for short periods of time. This troubled him. Herbs had failed to give her strength. He had summoned her family from her home in Acoma, New Mexico territory, a Sky Pueblo, she had not seen since her abduction by evil men whom he rescued her from. Still she grew weaker.

He now sought help from the only other source he knew, the Creator. His days had been long and his nights full of dreams. On one hand, he saw a baby being formed in the womb of the one he loved. On the other, he saw a large hand that was dirty trying to pull the baby from the safety of the womb. Troubled, he sought the answer to what this meant. Hunger tore at his stomach and weakness plagued him. Still, his thoughts remained unanswered.

The sound of laughing tormented his ears.

He rose abruptly and faced his enemy. "Fight, you foe from the unknown. Face me now," he cried.

The laughing grew louder as he swung his large knife in a half circle before him, cutting air as he swung it.

He sat as he had watched his grandfather do many times before him, facing east on a large stone. It was worn smooth from many others' use. He watched the sun return to the land of his people. He watched its journey, as the day grew long, continually asking audience with the Creator. As the sun prepared to embark and ready itself for the return of darkness, he climbed high upon the sacred mountain, glimpsing as long as possible the rays of sun reaching out to him. Still no answer filled his understanding. The shadows grew as darkness returned. Once again he sang the song of his people softly, at first, then louder. His songs continued well into the night. While others slept, his head slumped down as his spirit entered the dream world. He walked, bent over carefully as a hunter would, watching as if any moment an animal would burst forth revealing itself to him. He approached the place he had seen the riderless horse pass. He studied the earth for sign. Though the soil was soft, no tracks were made where the animal passed.

He cautiously approached the direction in which the shots were fired. He turned a bend in the canyon he followed. The sounds of men and animals working drifted towards him. He took cover in some bushes and crept closer to a vantage point. He could see four Mexicans working a large opening into the earth. They talked loudly to each other as they went about their business. One was by a small pool in the shade of willow trees panning the ore they were mining. This one called to the others and they hurried over to him. They gathered around smiling, obviously pleased at what they saw in the pan. The Indian could see the unmistakable glow of yellow metal as one of the men raised a nugget to look at it in the sun light. The Indian reached to his side and rested his hand on his large knife.

He moved closer to the Mexicans' diggings. He watched silently, seeking to find a weak spot in their defenses. A noise caught his attention, a sound of a woman's voice. He looked around trying to see who made the noise. Then he saw movement coming from the entrance of the mine. Bent over, a woman carrying a large basket full of ore appeared. As she dumped her load, she turned and faced his direction. It was a face he recognized, the face of.... Then his eyes caught movement behind the woman. A Mexican approached her from the shadows. He did not approve of her pausing for a moment to enjoy water and sunlight. He grabbed her by her hair and pulled her towards the mine. He cursed loudly as he pushed her into its entrance. When the man turned, the Indian saw his face clearly for the first time. The Indian's heart raced as he saw his eyes and his bent nose; they all looked familiar to him. He had seen them before high on a mesa overlooking the Salt River. He saw the others and recognized them as well, all he had killed and left their bones to be bleached by the sun. The woman was now his wife. What was she doing here? The four men were dead, yet they lived on in this world of dreams. They were still holding his wife hostage and using her to do their will, evil men much in need of killing again. His hand once more fell to his side and rested on his knife. He looked at his rifle and checked to see if it was ready. He rose to his feet and took a step towards the mine. He could not move. His muscles would not bend. It was as if a heavy weight rested upon him, holding him down. The Indian grew faint under this weight and soon darkness once again encircled him.

The campfire's warmth reached the young boy as he sat opposite his grandfather. A brisk breeze brought the damp cold air from the tops of the snow-covered mountains to their camp. While the cold ate at him and held him captive, his grandfather appeared to be comfortable.

"You see," the old man said as he watched the young boy shiver. "If you know the cold, it can have no power over you."

With that, he removed his shirt and splashed water over his chest. The rest of the evening, he remained shirtless.

"The cold is powerful," he said. "It brings the snow, the rain that gives life. All lives as a result of it. It truly is my friend." With that he stood and walked over to a smooth rock. He sat down cross-legged and began to sing ever so softly.

The young man strained his ears so he could hear. While the old man was thus involved, he stood up and removed his shirt to be like his grandfather. He did not stand far from the fire that night, but the words the Old One spoke stayed with him. He, too, walked the way the Old One did, with power and strength.

From the darkness that held him, his mind fought to regain control. From his youth, the teachings of his grandfather reached out to him. He knew fear; it had no power over him. He knew these four men. He had overpowered them once. He would fight on. He removed his shirt, and then gripped the leather bag around his neck. Inside, was black and white paint. With it, he colored his face, arms and chest. He reached down to his side and pulled his knife from its sheath. He rubbed his thumb down its blade softly, feeling its edge. It met his approval. He shoved it back into its place. His rifle lay on his back attached around his neck and under his arm ready, if need be.

He crawled on his belly, like a wolf, closer to the mine. The four men were busy at various stages of mining. The woman carried ore out of the mine and dumped it at its entrance. He tried to get her attention, but she turned and entered the mine without seeing him.

Suddenly hooves sounded from approaching riders. The Indian remained hidden in some bushes close to the mine's entrance. Several warriors of his people swooped down to steal the Mexicans' horses. One Mexican had a large gray horse tied close to the mine. He jumped into the saddle and gave chase towards the raiding party. An arrow, then another, arched upward into the air, then settled into a line towards him. One arrow hit him in the shoulder, knocking him to the ground. The other imbedded itself into the swell of the saddle as he was falling. The big gray horse headed down the canyon as many shots were being fired at the Indians by the remaining three Mexicans. This was the same horse Quintero had seen as he watched high above the canyon from his vantage-point. "The Great Spirit!" he said softly as he watched the animal disappear into the distance.

Hearing the gun shots, the woman cautiously approached the mine opening. Quintero saw her and rushed to put his arm around her to protect her. She started to pull away, as if she did not know him. From the corner of his eyes, he saw the man with the crooked nose running towards them. Quintero reached for his knife. His hand would not move. He saw a second Mexican quit shooting at the Indian raiding party and head towards them. He tried to position his rifle with his other hand. It, too, would not obey him.

"Woman!" he yelled loudly. "Take my knife and kill them!"

The woman took a step as if to outrun the Mexicans. Quintero stood firm, facing his enemy. This gave the woman determination to do the same. She grabbed the knife just as the Mexicans reached for her. It found the mark. It sank to the handle in his chest, and an instant later the second man tasted her blade, and lay dead at her feet.

Quintero awakened as the sun crept up from the east. He was on a large smooth stone, the one his grandfather also sat on many times. He looked around. His horse grazed in the distance. Black and white paint mixed with blood covered him. He felt his side; four deep scratches were there, his wife's fingernails left their mark as she clung to him. They were still bleeding. He collapsed back upon the rock.

It was warm now. The day must be partly over, he thought. The blood was dry. He went to the creek nearby and washed himself off. He hurried back to his horse, caught him and rode toward the east. A canyon he would recognize lay ahead. He rode below a point of rocks some distance above him, then up a bushy, narrow side pocket, once again entering into a large wash. He traveled for sometime up this wash before he saw what he was searching for. Then what appeared to be tailings from an old mine became noticeable; he headed to them. A mineshaft lay above the tailings. It appeared as if they were undisturbed.

Quintero dismounted and walked over to the mine entrance. Something shiny caught his eye. He walked to it and picked up his knife. He looked at it for a moment, then wiped the blood from it and put in its sheath. A length of cord lay on the ground by where the knife was laying. He recognized it as the rayeta that bound his wife that night above the Salt River. He bent over and picked it up. He pulled on it testing its strength; it broke easily. "She is free of them!" he thought as he remounted and rode for Metate Mound.

In the distance he heard a short yell, a cry he knew so well. "Grandfather!" he said softly.

The trip home was swift. Quintero was anxious to see his wife. Her time was at hand. He gave a loud yell as he rode across the Salt River.

Several relatives returned it as he entered his Rancheria.

"The baby is here!" one said, as Quintero dismounted his horse.

Quintero ran for his house. The woman smiled as she handed the man his son. It was then that he noticed the sandal he had found in the cave hanging in the doorway. Quintero looked at his wife; he could see a great change had come over her.

"Are you well, my wife?" he asked.

"It is so," was all she said.

He noticed her four broken finger nails as she handed him the child.

Life is to be lived, not necessarily understood, he thought, as he cradled the baby in his arms.

LUCKY BOY MINE
Chapter 14

The mule deer was pushing sixteen inches of snow trying to make its way to winter range in the valley below.

Steve Ivory had just came down off the Devils Backbone, a rugged ridge running opposite of Mt. Graham by Stockton Pass, Arizona Territory. He held a piece of high ground searching below him trying to find something to put on the dinner plate.

A winter storm front had come through this part of the country. Steve had been cabin bound for several days. He was lucky the last person to use the line shack had stocked plenty of wood in it. The stove had danced for the time he was held up in the shack, yet he still blew condensation with every breath. He was weak. Nothing was left of the meager stores he brought from town. Hunger had stalked him for the many days he had been cabin bound by the storm.

Finally, the sun had managed to show its way through the heavy clouds. Again, warmth was returning to the land. Steve saddled his horse and rode down the trail off the rough mountain toward home.

It was then he encountered the large mule deer buck heading out of the brush-choked ridges onto the floor of Bar X canyon. He figured if it continued the course it was traveling, he would get a chance to shoot it. Steve watched carefully as the deer approached him at an angle that would put it directly below him, well within range. He pulled his rifle from the scabbard on his horse, rested it on the largest rock, and held his breath. Just as he was about to pull the trigger, a shot rang out from the other side of the canyon. The deer dropped in its tracks. Steve Ivory rubbed his chin out of nervousness. He, as of yet, could not see who had fired the shot.

The Indian had been watching a buck move through the snow. Many days had came and gone since his last meal. He had made his way down the mountains of central Arizona to the Sonoran desert home of his people. He had held up at Metate Mound. The snow began in the evening and continued for two days. It reached the belly of his horse when he left early the final morning. The snow was not as much as he drew closer to Apache Canyon. He had spotted the deer by the sun shining off its antlers. Flashes of light reached his eyes as if being shown from a mirror. He left his horse tied to an oak bush some distance away. He snuck to an outcropping of rock looking down on the trail most likely the deer would use to continue on its way. One shot was all it took to fell the animal.

He went back to his horse and carefully led him towards the deer. It was then he looked ahead and saw the cowboy leading his horse to the deer as well.

Eyes alert to the smallest detail glared out of each face of the would be hunters. Steve Ivory began to walk in a clockwise direction around the deer. He had dropped his horse's rein and rested his hand on his pistol.

Quintero began to pace around the deer in the same direction as the cowboy, his rifle held on the ready. Each man glared at the other.

This continued until the snow was packed down in a large circle around the animal. Finally, the cowboy, Steve Ivory, began to laugh loudly. A puzzled smile hung on the lips of the Indian, Quintero.

"Hell's bells," Steve spoke through strained lips; "there's enough deer for both of us."

The Indian looked at him for a minute and began to laugh, too.

Steve reached for his knife and said, "It's your deer, but I'd be glad to help gut it for a piece of meat."

Quintero smiled and laid his gun against the forks in a small bush. Together they worked until the deer was roasting on a mesquite fire.

The sun began to make its disappearance as the two men sought shelter in a grove of cedar trees for the night. After a stab at small talk, Steve Ivory crawled into his bedroll and pulled his hat down over his face. His mind began to wander back to his youth, a time when he was known by a different handle. They called him "Lucky" back then. But like so many things that aren't what they seem, this was a hard and perilous time in his life...

He had been riding for an outfit on the Blue River, in and about the same area where the Three Mesas is now. He had left early in the morning to ride high on the canyon tops and look for the boss' prize bull, two days on the lam. He trailed him through brush thicker than hair on a hog's back, but lost his tracks on a stone floor that stretched in every direction. It was on the way home that he came upon a burro loaded with gold ore, almost pure, maybe alloyed with silver. The burro was standing in the trail eating on some brush. Tame enough, the burro let him catch and tie him up. After backtracking, it was clear to Steve the burro was traveling alone. The day was far spent so he led the burro back to the ranch. He figured he'd get a search party rounded up and look for the animal's owner first thing in the morning.

It was when he brought all that gold in and everyone saw it that he got the name "Lucky." It stuck for a while, he thought back, but it didn't do anything at all for his well being. Not a sign of the poor cuss who mined the gold was ever discovered. But human nature being what it is, rumors began to fly. Seems they allowed that he must have been doing some mining on the side. In fact, "The Lucky Boy Mine" was said to be somewhere north and east of Grasshopper Saddle. It was there that he hoarded the richest gold mine ever discovered.

After the gold was taken to Mineral Point in New Mexico to be sold, word spread fast to every drifter and hard case in the two-state area. It would only be a matter of time before someone came looking for the mine. Steve would often see them trailing him while he was punching cattle. Ash piles would betray the camp sites overlooking the headquarters of the ranch. Someone was keeping an eye on his comings and goings.

One day Steve was riding in late. He was alone. Four toughs blocked his way as he came around a rock outcropping.

"Pull up!" one said loudly.

Steve's horse reared up slightly as he fought to gain control. From the side of him, someone grabbed his horse's rein and, in the commotion, knocked him to the ground. Another threw a lariat around him and cinched him tight.

"Lucky boy! Where's your mine?" one yelled loudly as he began to pull him down the trail.

The others followed him along, laughing. When they came to a large ponderosa pine, the stranger threw the rope over a branch and pulled up the slack. Steve's feet, now just shy of the ground, sent him tumbling downward as the rope pulled tighter. Two men jumped from their horses and moved the loop up to his neck. The horsemen raised him off the earth, stopping his wind. They toyed with him for what seemed like forever.

Steve's life played before his eyes. Though still a boy by some standards, he had been doing a man's job most of his life. He had left home after his pa had been killed in the war. His mother just had too many mouths too feed, it seemed to him. Yet now, he wished he'd spent more time with a mother he hardly knew. Here in the rough parts of Arizona, a lucky find by chance, gold would be his undoing. A more appropriate name would be "Unlucky," he thought.

Steve woke up chilled. He felt himself to make sure he was unhurt. He began to rehearse in his mind the day's events. Near as he could tell, they tired of playing this deadly game and rode on. He told them over and over how he found the gold. Blinded by greed, they could not see he was telling them straight. They rode off leaving him for dead. It was morning by the time he walked to the ranch. A scar still ringed his neck where the rope burned him.

Now, as he lay on this frozen plain below the Devil's Backbone, not more than ten feet away, more than likely was the only man alive who knew the location where the gold on the burro he found came from. His grandfather probably did in the unfortunate miner up on the Blue River. Quintero, an Indian, had been trained by his grandfather, to seek out and hide all mines and any sign of gold in the lands of the Apache. This, his grandfather, also named Quintero, had done all of his life, too, before him.

Now this man lay at his side. "How fate plays a man," Steve thought; "two opposites if ever there were."

Steve had often left his job when he could to go back to the Three Mesas country and search for the mine. It was his thought that perhaps he had missed a small clue that would show him where the mine was. Now, a lifetime later, he rested with the grandson of the man he had often seen in the wilds of an earlier Arizona trying to hide the very thing he was looking for. He knew that this man's grandfather had shown him the location of this rich deposit. They would want to take extra precautions with such a rich deposit of gold. "Yes, he knows," Steve thought.

Morning found a bitter chill at Bar X canyon. The fire felt good as the men stood around it trying to thaw out after the cold night. They once again cooked flesh from the deer. Steve tried to get the Indian to talk a little but, as usual, he was met by silence.

The horses were caught and stood ready. Steve walked over to Quintero and asked him point blank if he knew where the gold he found up on the Three Mesas was mined. Quintero looked down at the snow, then raised his head and looked at the tiny shaft of sunlight breaking through the mountain pass.

Silent for a moment, then Quintero spoke; "Yes I know, I have been there many times."

Steve stood and watched the Indian disappear into the distance. To do more would have put him on the same level as the jaspers that tried to waylay him in his youth. Steve jumped on his horse and rode hard for Willcox. If lucky, he might be home before nightfall. "But, then again," he thought, "I never claimed to be lucky."

FATE HAS THE UPPER HAND
Chapter 15

Days come; they go, mostly offering at best, boredom to most. Yet, at times, days come thundering down on one as if to trample him by a hundred hoofs of runaway herds, of days since past, days not sorted and put to rest as should have been, but instead, left in disarray by chance, of things out of one's control. It is days such as this that come from one's past and stalk the present, in search of weakness, worry and pride--a place to grow and become a thorn in the orderly affairs of things, to bloom as trouble on the not too distant horizon.

It was on a day such as this that Steve Ivory saddled his horse, early before the sun had a chance to clear the summit of the Chiricahua Mountains. His dust would soon announce his departure from the village of Willcox, Arizona Territory. A search for gold lay ahead, or behind. He did not know for sure. Gold was like that. Clues from the past are the only trails leading to the present location of missing gold--a golden cross the Mexican called the "Cross of St. Stephen," all too often lost somewhere on some arid plains in the wake of death. The grave of Hector Antonne must be found, he thought, as he spurred his horse onward.

Señor Antonne had spent the winter at a hotel on Railroad Avenue in Willcox. His trail had often crossed that of Steve Ivory. A friendly acknowledgement of each other masked the true feeling of uncertainty each had for the other.

The days had begun to take on the feel of spring. And the hunger once again filled the Señor's bosom that would only be satisfied by the finding of the golden cross. Once it was so close to being in his hands, yet now lost once more, a condition all too familiar to his family. Señior Antonne's lungs had filled with fluid and almost cost him his life. He had been nursed back to health by several sympathetic souls able to cure the ill with herbs and sheer determination. He, once again, felt strength return to his frame and gold entered his dreams at night, his mind by day. "The golden cross must be protected by the lives of the Saints," he said under his breath. "It must not fall into the hands of the likes of Steve Ivory."

Quintero caught his horse and checked its feet. The stallion, well rested, had endured winter well. He was anxious to feel the horses' muscles working under him. To see the landscape change as he left the mountains he called home. Ahead lie the broad valleys of desert that was also home to him and to his people who, before him from time beginning, held this land from others until the Whites pushed them back to diverse places.

Ahead lay matters that caused him unrest, as winter's fury unfolded outside the walls separating him from the elements. Matters of importance were left undone, of promises made to the Old One, his grandfather, to find the golden cross that the Mexican Hector Antonne lost while returning to Mexico. His life had entwined with his grandfather's until friendship bound them together as brothers, then was taken away by the great hand of death, the hand of no escape. At this hour, the cross once more returned to the earth and remained so. Yet, a promise made to the Old One must be fulfilled, a promise to find and place the cross with other gold hidden from those who dug it in Apacheria. The bear and sacred feather of the Eagle should be set free from the container holding them captive in the base of the golden cross. It was grandfather's will. He would do his best to fulfill it. He must find the cross before someone else, he said to himself.

The horse broke into a run as it crossed the Salt River; the cold droplets of water found the Indian's face. He bent low to the animal's neck as he let it have its head. Winter's grip had finally been released from the land. The man and horse became one as they felt the rebirth of spring.

Steve Ivory knew this place well. The Dos Cabezas Mountains towered above him to the north, in the foothills below them the small mining town of Dos Cabezas stood; the Chiricahuas were to the east. The wash had received considerable flooding during the winter storms, yet the signs of fresh digging revealed that others were smitten with lust for the lost golden cross. Secrets were like that, he thought. Each, who hears, tells ten others and so on, until the whole earth knows, yet doesn't. The stones surrounding the fire pit were tossed aside and a hole stood agape, dirt piled high around it. Steve searched for the familiar mesquite tree and removed the saddle from his horse. He stored it under the tree and stretched his legs while getting a new perspective of the campsite where the cross lay hidden. He was in deep thought as the day lengthened and the shadows grew long. His mind retraced all the steps he had taken leading up to this day. Facts returned to mind that had not been recalled for a while. Yet, here on this spot, all things large and small might fit together and reveal the puzzle in its entirety, if only he could bring them together.

Darkness stalked him and found him returning to his makeshift camp. His bedroll was tossed beside his saddle. A can of beans and a couple of stale biscuits served as a meal.

Dreams filled his mind even though his body ached for rest. Yet, rest was not to be, for this place was full of mystery, of death and destruction, each longing to be resolved, allowing peace to again return.

Steve Ivory was startled by the sudden sound. His hand found cold steel and pushed his pistol out from under his covers. He had not, as yet, determined what had summoned him out of deep thoughts and rest. Then it came again. An owl in an oak tree sounded its familiar hoot. Steve pulled his hat over his face. Sleep found him sometime in the night.

Señor Antonne had not been on a horse since arriving in town. But this day, he concluded, would be the day to begin the search anew. By mid afternoon, he arrived at the site of the lost cross. Steve was on hand to welcome him.

"Señor Steve, you are always a man of surprises. At least I know you have not previously found the golden cross," Señior Antonne said as he jumped down from the horses back. "May I join you in camp, Señor Steve?"

"Please, Señor, join me!" Steve offered.

Señor Antonne was in no hurry. He had waited patiently, for years, for the return of the cross. He would continue to live each day as the one before. "In God's time," he often said, he would find the cross.

Steve was still the driven individual he had always been. He had no time for hesitation, so he searched hard and wide hoping to find something out of place which perhaps, if corrected, might shed light on his pursuit.

The Mexican, content to let the will of God be done, was quite willing to help. He made forays up and down the wash and surrounding hills. Undeterred by finding nothing of importance, he searched on. When local treasure hunters from Dos Cabezas became too bold and ventured too close, he did his best to run them off. Most left peacefully, while others made idle threats. Señor Antonne was determined if the cross were found, it would be by him. Determined men usually have backbone to support them. None were inclined to call his hand, so the cross remained protected.

Quintero circled the ridges above the dry waterway. He saw the camp of the two men below him. Señor Antonne grabbed his rifle and held it on the Indian as he entered the wash and rode towards their camp. Steve Ivory saw the approaching rider from a distance as he returned from a day of searching. As he drew closer, he recognized the horseman. The Indian acknowledged Steve, then looked in the Mexican's direction.

"This here is Señor Antonne, Hector's uncle. This is Quintero," Steve said, as he looked at the Indian.

Señor Antonne laid his rifle aside.

"This fella's grandfather was with Hector when he took lead," Steve added.

"They were brothers," Quintero corrected.

"Then, perhaps you know where the cross is located?" asked Señor Antonne.

"No!" said Quintero. "My grandfather could not find it."

Steve eyed him suspiciously from a distance. Señor Antonne offered the Indian a meal and a place to camp. Quintero accepted his hospitality, looking over at Steve Ivory. He could not read anything in Steve's eyes, so

Quintero threw his gear upon the ground to the side of the camp and turned his horse to graze along with the others.

Three men, each motivated by a different cause, were all different, yet seeking a common object. Each had his own intention on what to do with it when found. Each was searching the other's words and actions, seeking any sign of betrayal of information concerning the golden cross. Measuring each other, pondering to what lengths the other was capable of taking to possess it. Yet, they shared a common bond of hospitality around a campfire, a neutral spot in a desolate corner of the earth. They were strangers, yet friends, until that hour when a shaft of light would illuminate a dull yellow glow and turn it into a burning inferno capable of consuming anything and everything.

Quintero had little use for Steve Ivory. He had seen him many times in different parts of Arizona. The day might come when they stood on different ends of a gun. Quintero had his idea about things, Steve Ivory another. The way Quintero had it figured, Steve Ivory wanted the golden cross for personal gain.

The Mexican, Señor Antonne, was another matter. He was here to further the quest for returning the cross to Mexico. Quintero reasoned that perhaps if his grandfather were still alive, he might feel compassion towards him considering the closeness he had with Hector. Still it was not for him to say what the Old One might have done. Today was today. He must act alone in deciding these things.

The following evening Quintero returned to the camp of the two men. He was able to find the grave of Hector Antonne. His grandfather had hidden it well. It was directly below a small mountain to the east of the wash where the robbery occurred. His saddlebags full of his belongings were hidden under some rocks by the grave. Everything was just as his grandfather had said they would be. He handed the bags to Señor Antonne, then turned his horse loose with the others.

Señor Antonne must have known what they were when he saw them. Silence encased him, and he spent the rest of the evening reading through a small book containing Hector's notes. He was happy momentarily and then, once again, sadness would show itself on his face. Quintero and Steve Ivory left him to his thoughts.

The following morning, Steve Ivory left at first light. He picked up the trail of the Indian. It was easy enough to follow. It made a long circle back to where he had come from. He entered the wash in a narrow steep and brushy place. It was when he exited the other side that he found Quintero sitting on his horse waiting for him. Quintero did not speak to him, but his eyes said plenty. He rode his horse across the trail blocking the way. Steve Ivory held up and turned his horse aside. The Indian would not yield. Steve saw his hand resting on one of the large knives on his belt.

"O.K., my friend!" Steve said coolly. "I understand." He kicked his horse's flanks and headed in a direct route to camp. "Once again I have been outfoxed," thought Steve, as he put distance between him and the Indian.

Camp was but a short distance ahead. Señor Antonne was still there, perhaps waiting; knowing this day was the day of change. No longer could he, Steve Ivory, stay in the middle and hope to remain unnoticed. He must choose which road he would use, for one would surely betray him. The other might afford a way for him to obtain the cross. Trying to trail the Indian had been a mistake. He had tipped his hand. Now Señor Antonne and Quintero would both know he was acting alone. He should have been more patient, he thought.

Señor Antonne could see there was no more doubt. He must watch Steve Ivory more carefully. "He is a coyote, a cunning one at that who would gladly have the cross for himself," thought Señor Antonne. "It will not happen. The cross is more than a piece of gold, it is a part of history to be kept for the believers, not just for the whims of a few chosen rich." Yes, it was his place to see that the golden cross remained in the hands of the church, and then his family's honor once more would be restored.

When Quintero returned to camp, the sun was but silver in the horizon. He noticed Steve Ivory had pulled out.

"Left early this morning. Said he was headed into town," Señor Antonne confirmed.

"When the sun rises tomorrow, we ride to Hector's grave," Quintero said.

"Yes, I'd like that!" Señior Antonne replied. "I read his notes last night. He had written several entries about your grandfather. Seems they were very close. I believe you now when you say you do not know where the cross is hidden. But where can it be?"

The Indian stared into the fire as if trying to find an answer himself. Señor Antonne fussed with the dinner utensils. The rest of the evening was spent in silence as the two men, each in his own way, searched for answers.

"Steve Ivory!" Mary said loudly as he entered the door to her café. "I was beginning to worry about you!" She wiped her hands on her apron as she walked towards him. She threw her arms around his neck. "It really is you, isn't it?" she grinned.

"Things didn't go the way I had them figured," Steve replied. "Anything to eat in this place? Been a while since I had any real cooking. Besides, I want a good look at you," Steve added.

"And I wouldn't mind getting a good look at you. That beard hasn't seen a razor since you left town."

Steve rubbed his chin for a minute as if acknowledging the truthfulness of his wife's words. "Are the boys in school?" he asked.

"Yes!" she replied. "They will be home soon, though."

"I'll be waiting for them," he said as he walked toward the door.

"Don't I get a tip today, cowboy?" she asked.
"That will be later!" he said with a grin.
She threw a hand towel his direction as he left the doorway.

The two men left camp early, their destination, a grave thought lost by Señor Antonne. It was with mixed emotion that he anticipated the gravesite. He wanted to find peace with Hector's death. Yet, uncertainty surrounded the loss of the golden cross, as well as his nephew's life. It was while thus engaged in deep thought, a shot rang out from the ridge top. The first bullet blew sand up at the feet of his horse. The horse was startled and began to crow hop. Señor Antonne fought to regain control of the animal. A second shot rang out and clipped his leg. It then passed into the horse, sending it and him to the ground. Quintero took shelter in nearby rocks. It was from this vantage point he saw the puff of smoke each time a shot was fired. Two more shots rang out hitting the earth around the Mexican. His leg remained pinned under the horse. So escape was impossible.

The ambusher, getting bolder with each shot, spent more time exposing himself. Quintero took a fine bead on the attacker as he was preparing to shoot again. One shot was all it took to teach the hombre a lesson, a lesson too late to do him any good.

Señor Antonne was a lucky man. He had a deep flesh wound, but his leg bone was unharmed. Sore indeed, he discovered as he tried to stand.

"My fate could have been the same this day as my nephew's had it not been for you. I owe you my life," said Señor Antonne.

The Indian smiled, but said nothing. He helped the Mexican hobble over to the gravesite.

While Señor Antonne sat on a large rock, Quintero scaled the mountain towards the dead man. Questions formed anew in the minds of the two men. "Would Steve Ivory stoop to this?" The soil had sunk outlining the grave. Time had allowed that. Señor Antonne fought to hold back tears as he sat beside Hector's resting-place.

Quintero was relieved to see the face of a stranger on the dead man. Even though he had differences with Steve Ivory, he hadn't figured him to be a man to ambush another. He found the man's horse, dropped its saddle and turned the animal loose. If this hombre has someone close, they will be back here looking for him when the horse returns home.

Quintero found Señor Antonne ready to return to camp. The big stallion carried both of them the short distance with ease.

Señor Antonne had a change of mind come over him and decided he had done all he could there. It was while looking down on the grave of Hector, and being shot in the leg, following his winter-long bout of pneumonia that he had come to know the bounds of human mortality. If the ambusher had been a better shot, Señor Antonne would have joined Hector in the earth. This did not matter, except for the fact that this was a strange land. His years being many, he preferred to find death in the company of his family in Mexico. The cross would have to wait for another family member, a younger one, to return to carry on the quest. In the afternoon, Quintero took the Mexican to Willcox and said farewell. He spurred the stallion and turned him in the direction of Metate Mound.

Quintero knew danger could be stalking him. If someone searched for the dead man, they could very well be following his trail at this moment. He made several large circles and stopped and waited to see if anyone trailed him. The third day rain came. It brought cold, yet relief. His tracks were no longer visible in the soft earth. He sought shelter among the rocks. It was dry there, and he built a small fire to keep him warm. His mind wandered and retraced the events of late. The man who attacked them must have been watching them, perhaps, for days. He must have been seeking the golden cross. "How many more will die?" he asked himself.

The morning broke clear, the horse had wandered up the canyon in search of food. He, likewise, was in need of nourishment. He followed the horse's tracks until he found him. He whistled and the horse came to him. On the ridge above, grazed several of the White's buffalo. "How easy it would be to kill one of the tame animals," he thought. He did not see how they could survive in this place--a place where the deer run like the wind, yet still become food for the lion and bear.

He jumped on the horse and crowded him down the wash. At the cave he gathered his belongings and once more rode towards Metate Mound. What had once been many, now yielded only a few pieces of jerky. He must find some game this day or remain hungry from here on.

He could see the Fort at the base of the mountain. His destination lay a short distance to the west. Once there, he would stalk for game. The Spirit of his people was there. They would guide him to the trail of the wary deer or antelope.

Evening found him cooking the flesh of a rabbit. "It is enough," he thought, as he sucked the meat from the bones. Hunger had been defeated once more, a ritual that was played over and over each day. If he won, he ate. If unsuccessful, he remained hungry. This day his luck remained strong.

Many days passed; nights filled with prayers came and went. His direction remained unfocused. He could not understand how he was to find the golden cross. On the final evening that he was to spend at Metate Mound, he sprinkled corn meal in the four directions and took the seat of the ancients. It was cold, yet an old friend. He began to sing, to summon the Creator and ask for his help, as he could not do this on his own. It was late, it was early; he did not know. But a dream found him. A large black boar bear stood on its hind legs sniffing the air. It looked as if it was in search of a bear cub to eat as they often do. An eagle circled overhead watching the mighty bear. The bear's nose went to the ground, searching a wide area, stopping often to rise on its hind legs and look around. Quintero could see the mountains behind the large wash the bear hunted in; they were the Dos Cabezas. The eagle rose in an updraft higher and higher into the sky, looking as if was above the mountains. In time, the bear found his way to the place where the golden cross was lost. Under a mesquite bush behind a large boulder the bear stopped. Again he stood up sniffing the air. Then he dropped back on all of his feet. At this time he began to dig under a mesquite tree, one swipe after another, the earth was torn open. The eagle landed in a large cedar tree to watch the bear dig. All at once the golden cross rolled out of the hole, its contents spilling upon the ground. The stone bear, once inside the cross, grew before his eyes and turned into a larger bear than the first. It showed its teeth then drove the first bear from view. The eagle flew down by the cross and picked up the single feather and leather string, and flew off after the bear. Quintero felt as if he was standing above watching the bear and eagle. The cross lay in the freshly dug earth. He saw the sun sparkling off the green stones.

Morning came and brought with it the bright sunlight. It burned Quintero's eyes as it made its appearance. He looked around to see where he was. "Metate Mound," he whispered to himself. After finding his horse and gathering his belongings, he rode for Dos Cabezas. Time was of the utmost importance; he was sure now where the cross was.

Steve Ivory did not like how his search ended. He was outfoxed by Quintero and longed to settle the score. He had a few facts of his own and was determined to see them through. It was a hasty exchange of farewells between him and his family. He felt an urgency to return to Dos Cabezas. He saddled his horse and rode out of town. He entered the wash sooner than he usually did. The tracks of a large bear caught his interest and led him into the wash. He could see where the bear had dug a large hole under a mesquite tree. Upon riding closer, he saw the glow of the golden cross.

"Never before have I seen anything of such beauty!" he said loudly.

In one sweep of movement, he was off his horse gathering the cross in his hands. A small cap lay beside it in the dirt. He looked inside the cavity. "Empty," he said to himself. It was then he noticed the stone bear with an eagle feather tied to it, laying on the fresh dirt beside the golden cross. He bent over, retrieved them and put them into his shirt pocket. Suddenly, he found himself looking about to see if anyone was watching him. Reassured, he wrapped the cross in his bedroll and led the horse the short distance to the mesquite tree where he camped.

Steve Ivory thought it wise to once again hide the golden cross for safekeeping. This time he buried it close to his bed so he could keep an eye on it. Soon a fire was crackling; food was placed to cook on the rocks around the fire. No longer in a hurry, Steve Ivory thought he might as well enjoy a good meal.

The sun had hardly cleared the mountaintops the following morning when the shots began. Narrowly escaping death, Steve barrel rolled until he reached the safety of the nearby rocks. Many more shots followed. Steve had a hard time returning fire as they had him pinned. For the moment he was watching his backside, thinking they might circle him. Movement caught his eye. His gun in one instant became an extension of his arm pointing at the intruder.

"Quintero!" Steve whispered. "You're a welcome sight."

"Came to give you a hand," the Indian replied. "I know where they are. I could see them as I came in. When I get across this thicket, fire a couple of rounds to keep them looking your way."

With that, Quintero resumed his stalk. He crawled unnoticed among the bushes. When he reached his position, Steve did as requested. Three quick shots toward the ambushers were followed by several from Quintero. Cries of pain announced that death was present. Now that they had them in the crossfire, Steve Ivory joined in. Two more men were put down by flying lead. A fifth man died as Quintero's knife found him. The remaining three men retreated to their horses.

"What are they after?" Steve asked softly.

"The last time I was here, Señor Antonne and I were shot at, a man wounded the Señor, so I killed him. They must be seeking revenge," said Quintero.

"Just my luck," said Steve, "to stumble into a hornet's nest."

The two men stayed hidden in the rocks watching the retreating men.

"Suppose they might be back?" Steve asked.

"Might!" Quintero replied.

The sun was high overhead; still no sign of the ambushers. Steve Ivory made his way cautiously over to his grub sack and canteen. He then hurried back to the rocks. As Steve bent over to set them down, the stone bear fell from his pocket onto the ground.

"Where did you get this?" Quintero demanded.

Steve did not have time to say anything before the Indian jumped him. The two men rolled onto the ground in combat. One, then the other was on top. Quintero raised his knife and held it against Steve's throat.

"Where is it!" he yelled. "I know you have the cross."

Steve remained silent. This spurred the Indian into more of a rage. He raised his knife higher, readying it to plunge into Steve. A shot sent Quintero's arm hanging useless by his side. Steve pushed Quintero aside while firing his gun. A quick shot sent the intruder folding over. The two remaining men, seeing their friend lying dead, headed into the thick brush for safety.

Quintero's arm bled profusely. He would die if the flow of blood were not stopped. Steve worked quickly. He grabbed a piece of cloth and pushed it into the wound. Applying pressure, the flow lessened.

"You would save the life of one who would have killed you?" Quintero asked.

"You would not of carried it out," returned Steve.

"You do not know for sure," the Indian replied.

After remaining silent for a while, the Indian cautiously addressed Steve once more. "What will you do with the cross?" Quintero asked.

Steve had been searching the dead man trying to find out who he was and possibly where he was from. He had returned to camp with several of his possessions. He was studying some of the papers he found.

"Can you read them?" Quintero asked.

"Sure I can!" Steve lied.

"What do they say, then?" The Indian asked.

"Can't see it plainly; I don't have my eye piece with me."

"Oh!" said Quintero.

Steve folded the paper and put it deep in his pocket; he would show it to Mary later.

"You didn't answer my question," Quintero said once again.

"I will keep it!" said Steve.

"How will you keep it, my friend? Already many have died around it; perhaps you are next!"

"I'll take my chances then. I will not give it up."

"What about Señior Antonne?" Quintero inquired.

"He has gone back to Mexico. I saw him board a train myself."

"He will send another family member and another. He is a determined man." Quintero knew he had said enough. He remained quiet for awhile, then once more chose his words carefully and spoke again.

"The cross is but gold," Quintero said.

"You speak as one who has no need for gold, and so you are. I have plenty of need for it. In the White's world, gold is money. With it, everything is possible," Steve said.

"There is plenty of gold," Quintero returned.

"For you maybe, not for me." Steve Ivory challenged.

"Yes, for you. Have you forgotten the mine on Grasshopper Ridge?" said Quintero.

"I remember it well," Steve returned.

"There is plenty of gold there."

"What do you mean?"

"Just give me the golden cross," Quintero said matter of factly.

"You forget one thing. I could not find the Lucky Boy Mine."

"You will with my help. We leave as soon as my arm mends. The cross is beautiful, but the nuggets of gold at the mine are plentiful, many times the weight of the cross."

Steve Ivory could not find sleep that night. Too much was going on in his mind. First the cross, now this. He would consider the Indian's offer.

Neither man spoke again for awhile; then Steve Ivory broke the silence. "You would pay such a high price for the golden cross? Why is this so?"

"To fulfill a promise and make right something wrong. In time we will ride to look at the Lucky Boy Mine," finished Quintero.

WINK
CHAPTER 16

The Irishman was anxious to close the last few miles between him and home. The trip to Willcox was long and dusty. While there, he received word that was very exciting. Wink, her husband and child were coming home for a visit. Could it possibly have been the five years she claimed she had been away? The Irishman could hardly believe it. They had been happy years for him, yet the visit of his daughter would fulfill a hope he secretly held inside. He was just plain lonesome for his daughter. Letters he had received, from time to time, led him to believe she was the same. Maybe it was the years he spent searching for gold, leaving his loved ones behind in Ireland that made him long for his stepdaughter. Now, he wanted to be around those he loved to make up for all the lost years.

The horses knew home lay ahead. He gave them the reins and they hurried onward. Turning the corner around the rock point brought his home into view. The barking of the dogs called his wife to the front porch. A smile on her face welcomed him.

"Any mail this week?"

"Yes, my dear, and you won't believe the news! Wink is coming home. She will be here this Friday. The telegram said she will arrive by the afternoon train."

The woman's hands went up to her mouth as she gasped with excitement. "Come inside and read the telegram with me." They both hurried to the table, lit the lamp and sat down. It was passed back and forth several times.

"Yes, my dear," the woman finally said. "Your wish is going to be granted."

"How did you know?" he asked.

"I know more than you think I do!" she replied.

"I must admit I have missed her dreadfully, but I didn't want to burden you with it," the Irishman replied.

"Nothing you could say or do would be a burden for me. Just bringing me here to this beautiful place has brought me more happiness than I ever dreamed of."

"And you the same. You were worth the wait and hardship I endured." They sat and held hands for a moment. Then the man excused himself and went outside to do the chores.

The woman was fussing with some things in the kitchen when she heard the door open and once again the footsteps of her husband. She was surprised at his sudden return. He could not have possibly finished his work by now, she thought.

"Light me a lantern quickly while I get my gun!" he said.

"What's wrong?" she asked concern showing on her face.

"I don't know yet, but I think someone is in our barn and it looks like an Indian's horse tied to the fence. Don't come outside until I call for you!" he said as he turned away.

"You be careful!" she added as the door closed.

It was not long until the man's voice once again sounded loudly, "Come out here quickly!"

The door parted somewhat as the woman listened from the other side.

"Bring some hot water, and get something to bandage up a large wound. An Indian man has been shot and fever has rendered him unconscious."

The woman lost no time in doing as she had been instructed. One look at the Indian convinced her of the seriousness of the situation. The wound had been neglected and infection now threatened to claim this man's life. The Irishman cut the crude wrappings from the wound on the Indian's arm. The woman bathed the injured arm with soap and hot water. A poultice was prepared from bread and milk. She applied it to the wound and once more it was bound up tightly with bandages. Next, the two placed cold rags on his forehead and neck. They changed them repeatedly, trying to bring his temperature down. This proved to be an all night vigil.

Finally, the Irishman sent his wife into their house to get some rest. He made his bed on the floor close to the Indian and watched for any change on the sick man's face. The best he could possibly do was keep him comfortable and see what happened.

Morning brought the woman back to the barn. The Indian was still unconscious. The Irishman had fallen asleep sometime in the early hours. He woke at the sound of his wife's arrival. Once again they stripped the bandages from the man's arm. The poultice was drawing out some of the poisons. The woman put more of the same on the wound and bandaged it once more. The Irishman followed his wife back into the house. He had breakfast, then took care of the morning chores. They made some broth and returned to the barn. They took turns spooning tiny drops of the liquid into the injured man's mouth.

Toward evening, the Indian stirred. The Irishman was startled by the sound of his movement. He stood up and hurried towards the Indian and held his hands over his chest to prevent him from getting up. "Stay still where you are," he said gently. The man's eyes followed him, eyes that did not show fear, but of need. As the Irishman continued to work soaping a harness, the Indian's eyes once more closed and remained so the rest of the day.

The woman returned to the barn at evening and cared for the sick man once more. His eyes opened surveying his surroundings. He watched the woman tending his wound. More broth was offered the Indian. He drank freely of the large cup. The poultice had drawn more of the infectious poisons from the wound. The swelling had decreased and his fever had broken.

"After much rest, the Indian should recover," the Irishman said to his wife.

The following morning, the Irishman hitched up his team and was making ready to go into Willcox and wait for the arrival of Wink and her family. Excitement was in the air, yet the Irishman was hesitant to leave his wife alone with the injured man.

"I'll be alright," she assured him. "I'll stay in the house all day and keep busy. Time will pass quickly."

The Irishman pulled the watch from his pocket. At the same time he heard the faint whistle of the approaching train. "Forty five minutes late," he said under his breath; "not too bad."

The ground began to shake as the train grew closer. Minutes later, it came to a screeching halt blowing steam from its brakes. The conductor jumped off the train and lowered the steps. Soon, people were coming out of it. They dispersed in various directions. The Irishman began to feel a hint of discouragement building. Then his eyes caught a glimpse of the smile so familiar to him. "Wink!" he said loudly as she exited the train. He ran to offer his hand as she descended the short stairway. Her husband followed carrying a small bundle, which contained their son.

The father and daughter held each other tight, trying to catch up for the five years they had been apart. Then the Irishman broke the silence.

"You've returned to me. I always knew you would."

"Yes, father, I've missed you so much!" They stepped back to get a good look at each other.

"You look beautiful, my child," the father said.

Wink looked at her father and said that he hadn't changed a bit.

"You flatter me, my daughter," the Irishman returned.

Next, the Irishman went to the baby. "What a handsome boy!" he said. He offered a firm handshake to the father. "Congratulations on such a wonderful child are in order," he said.

They walked the short distance to the waiting wagon. The luggage was retrieved and with a jerk on the reins the wagon began to move. A magnificent sunset held them spellbound as the distance between them and the ranch narrowed. Quail flushed from cover along the road, when the wagon came to close to the trees they were gathering to roost in. Things the Irishman took for granted held his daughter spellbound. Occasionally. she would settle on something and speak excitedly about seeing it again after so long. The mountains, the broad expanses, desert plants, the dry washes, each had their turn to be rediscovered by an anxious Wink. The ranch came into view as they rounded the final curve. Wink asked her father to stop for a minute.

"It's just as I remembered," she said. She turned to her husband and said, "This is my home." A small bit of moisture glistened in the corner of her eyes.

Her father felt proud of how excited she was at the sight of the ranch house. He shook the reins and the wagon's wheels began to roll the final distance.

His wife greeted them on the front porch. She took turns embracing Wink and her nephew and the baby. The smile on her lips radiated the love she felt for the new arrivals.

Dinner was in the oven and ready to be served. While Wink freshened up somewhat, her husband and his "Auntie," as he called her, readied the table. The meal was excellent prime beef they had raised. Vegetables from the garden and fresh biscuits from the oven added the finishing touches.

The two Irishmen retired to the front porch. The younger man pulled cigars from his pocket and passed one to the other man. Soon smoke filled the air.

"Fresh from Cuba," Wink's husband added as he exhaled his first draw.

"What a pleasant surprise your visit is to the wife and me."

"Wink would not postpone it for another season."

"How long will you be staying?" the father inquired.

"I fear that it could be for sometime. Wink is not happy in Ireland, yet my life is there. My means of support will surely fail in my absence."

The Irishmen remained silent as each enjoyed his cigar. Finally the Irishman stood up and announced he had better do his chores. It was then he remembered the Indian in the barn in need of his help. He went into the kitchen and talked with his wife about their patient.

Wink, overhearing their conversation, inquired about the injured man,

"One of the local savages got shot in the arm," the woman replied.

"Auntie," Wink said, "you make him sound so distant, so detached from the rest of us. Have you forgotten, I am from the same blood?"

"Oh, my dear child, I mean no harm. And I certainly don't think as you and him being the same. You are our family; let us not stand divided. We have done our best to care for this man. He will soon be up and on his way," the woman finished.

The Irishman followed by his wife left the kitchen. Each carried supplies to care for the man. At the sound of the two entering the barn, the Indian's eyes opened. He smiled slightly at the two.

"I see you are awake; how do you feel?"

The Indian looked away, not revealing if he understood what the man was saying.

The Irishman drew closer and asked, "Do you understand what I'm saying?"

The Indian turned his head toward the couple and said, "I understand."

"Good," said the Irishman. "Now tell me how you are feeling this lovely evening."

"I shall ride soon."

"Not so fast," said the Irishman. "You are going to rest a few more days to make sure you are strong enough. Now, eat this food we have for you."

They watched him as he ate.

"His appetite has surely returned," the woman said.

After dressing his wound with a fresh bandage, the two returned to their house.

Wink followed her father as he went to look after the wounded Indian the next morning. Curiosity had built in her mind since the night before; she longed to satisfy it. When her eyes adjusted to the darkness of the interior of the barn, she got her first look at the Apache man. It had been many years since her childhood, yet she still vividly remembered. Yes, he looked just as she thought he would. The coarse hair, the high cheekbones, dark eyes, and red skin. She stared for a moment then turned and went back the way she came. Perhaps she noticed him returning her stare.

Quintero was equally curious as to where this beautiful Indian woman came from who dressed as a White. Then he recalled the girl raised by the Irishman, an Apache like himself, in fact, a distant cousin of his. They were from the same band that used to frequent this area, before changes came. The Irishman gave him food and drink, then went about caring for the animals.

Quintero's mind would not rest. He continued to think about the young woman. She was the most beautiful thing his eyes had ever seen. None could compare with her. He desired her, to feast on her beauty, to drink of words falling from her lips, to feel the breeze on his face as he walked beside her. He must find a way to gain her attention.

As the days came and went, Wink became accustomed to the routines about her. As night befell them, she offered to take the food and water to the Indian. A look of worry showed on her father's face for a moment. She saw it and reassured him she would be all right. She shut the door behind herself as she left the kitchen.

Quintero was pleased when he saw Wink. He spoke to her in Apache, but she showed no signs of recognition. He switched to English. "Thank you!" he said.

She smiled back at him and turned to walk away.

"Must you go so soon?" Quintero asked.

She once again faced him. "What is it you desire of me?" she asked.

"May I ask you a few questions?" Quintero replied.

"Alright," is all she said, eyes betraying her curiosity.

"I remember you as a child, when we were both young," Quintero continued. "We played in Apache Canyon with the other children, in the fallen rocks at the narrows. The sun reflecting from the large rocks kept us warm on the cold days. Do you remember?"

"I have had these thoughts before. I believed they were dreams put there at night."

"No, they were real, things that happened when we were still a people," Quintero said.

She paused for a moment then asked, "What is your name?"

"Little Bear," he replied. "Since becoming a man I have taken the name of Quintero, after my grandfather."

"Little Bear, I have heard such a name. I will think on these things and try to recall. I must leave you now, we will talk again."

Quintero had no mind for food. It was a hunger for the sight of this woman that burned in his stomach. The fact that she was Apache, yet knew little of the Apache ways, called out to him. He desired to lead her back to a path of knowledge, a path she came from, a path to him.

Quintero knew the time was at hand for him to leave. To stay longer was to impose upon these people. He would have none of that. Wink brought him his evening meal. Words came hard for him. "I will leave in the night," he said to her. "Please pass on my gratitude to your parents. My life was saved by them."

"Where will you go?" Wink asked.

"I will stay a few days at Apache Canyon. Then I will ride for home to my family. Will you visit me again before I go?" Quintero wanted to know.

"Yes," she sighed. Her eyes once again expressed a look of curiosity.

"Good," he said, "until then, goodbye."

She left the barn without looking back.

Many Apache men have more than one wife, Quintero reasoned, though the custom was dying out. Still with some it continued. He was able to provide for another woman and if the opportunity came he would pursue it. It would not alter in any way his love for his wife and child at home. It would just extend his family ties a little further. Rest found him a willing captive.

Before the first light, he was astride his horse riding the short distance to Apache Canyon. A spring lay at its head in some rocks. He would rest here a few more days. Soon his strength would return to him. Then many things must be accomplished. Yet, the woman occupied most of his thoughts.

A frame of logs stood where someone had built a shelter in the past. It would be easy to cut some cedar boughs and cover it. He worked short periods of time, then rested. By doing so he had the shelter finished by nightfall. He rigged a few deadfalls and snares in hope of capturing food. He had saved crusts of bread and other tidbits of food the Irishman had given to him. He hid it, knowing he would need something to keep him until he could provide for himself. Now it would sustain him until his traps began to yield.

Two days passed without seeing another person. On the third day, Wink came riding up the canyon. She halted by the rocks where they had played as children. Quintero walked the short distance to her. She held out to him a small bundle of food she had brought. Quintero accepted it and asked her to stay and visit. They walked among the rocks, she commenting on various things that she recalled. She told him how different this place was compared to Ireland.

"Where is Ireland?" he asked.

"It is one of the far away lands across the ocean, where the Whites came from." She told of spending many years there with her husband.

With this revelation, Quintero could not hide his disappointment.

She noticed the change and tried to convince him of the sincerity of her friendship, but that her main interest lay in the fact of their common ancestry.

A smile once more returned to the Indian's face.

Wink grabbed his hand and squeezed it gently. She turned and walked towards her horse.

He watched as she made her way down the valley and disappeared in the distance.

The following days were filled with visits from Wink, each lasting longer than the previous. Quintero taught her stories of Apache life--of birth, of death, of joy and sadness. Of Mangas Colorado, Cochise, and Geronimo. Of the creation, of customs and seasons. There was so much to share, with one who was willing to learn; yet they had so little time.

Quintero gave Wink the stone bear and eagle feather. He had kept it the day Steve Ivory dropped it from his pocket. It would once more belong to a special woman. He carefully placed the leather cord around her neck.

"I don't know what to say," stumbled from Wink's lips.

He heard the rider coming. He thought it to be Wink. He was wrong, the Irishman instead rode into his camp. His words put Quintero on the defensive.

"You there, be gone, or I'll dust your seat with buckshot."

Quintero knew this day would come. He wished inside it needn't be, but come it did. He dropped his hand to his side. It found his knife just in case. He didn't want to harm the Irishman; yet sometimes it got down to kill or be killed. The man walked closer, the double barrel looking straight into Quintero's eyes.

"Leave my daughter alone!" he said.

The Indian weighed each word coming from the man's mouth. Finally he said, "She is Apache first, your daughter after that."

"No!" the Irishman offered. "She is my ward."

"Yes, that is true, but she was first Apache. It is she who seeks her beginnings, not I who sought her out."

The dust on the horizon announced another rider would soon join the two men. Quintero could see it was Wink. The Irishman, as of yet, did not know his daughter was approaching. Thundering hooves changed all of that. As she turned her horse to bring him under control, she yelled, "Father, what are you doing?"

"I came to save your marriage, child."

"Quintero knows I am a married woman," Wink said. She jumped from her horse and walked towards the two men. As she approached, they both cautioned her not to get between them.

"For your safety," the Irishman pleaded.

Quintero backed up a few paces to put some distance between him and the Irishman. Wink still occupied the middle ground. The Indian would not endanger the woman so he continued to back up.

"Go home, father!" Wink shouted. "I am a grown woman. I can take care of myself."

The Irishman lowered the side by side, rejection showing upon his features. He walked back to his horse. Securing the reins he found the saddle and spurred the animal. The ranch lay beyond two ridges.

Wink had never spoken to her father before in such a tone. His shock and disbelief showed through his masked face. She would make it up to him later. For the present, two stubborn men had been saved.

A RIDE INTO UNCERTAINTY
Chapter 17

Quintero knew he must ride soon. So much hinged upon what he had to do. An offer had been made to the cowboy, Steve Ivory, an offer to take him to the Lucky Boy Mine. Quintero thought it strange how they both wanted something so badly, he, the golden cross, and the cowboy's interest lie in the mine. Neither was content with what they had.

Now complications in the form of a beautiful woman slowed Quintero down. A woman who he would gladly have as his own, yet impossible. Still the thought tasted delicious in his mind.

Wink rode into Quintero's camp as she had done so many times. She was not greeted by the usual warm smile from the Indian's lips.

"What is wrong?" she asked.

"Nothing is wrong. I must soon be on my way."

"Where will you go?" she inquired.

"I will ride north several days. There at my journey's end is a rich gold mine."

"What would you need gold for?" Wink asked.

"I do not need it," Quintero volunteered. "A man has something of great value I must purchase with it."

"I do not understand," Wink added.

"You will one day," Quintero quieted her.

The Indian solemnly looked into Wink's eyes. He stared deeply into them, searching for answers. She grew discomforted by his behavior and asked him what troubled him, once more.

"Can I trust you?" he asked.

"I was wondering the same about you," she replied.

"What do you mean?" he asked.

"You are a man, I am a woman. Need I say more? My mind hungers to learn of our people, yet I know the needs of a man."

Quintero, silent for a moment in thought, then replied, "Yes, you can trust me."

The woman smiled at his humility, then added: "You may trust me also."

"I must ride soon to the gold mines. Will you accompany me?"

"I don't know," she said as she fought to comprehend what he was saying. After a long silence, she said: "Yes, I will go!"

Wink did not enjoy the thought of what she must do. Her husband would not understand the importance she placed on riding with, Quintero. She felt as if her life lay waiting to be discovered. Still she knew she owed her husband more than this. Yet, words seemed shallow at the moment, unable to convey her true feelings. Feelings of love yet complicated by a desire to find her beginnings.

"I will be gone for a few days," she finally blurted out over breakfast.

"What do you mean?" her husband inquired.

"I have decided to join Quintero on a ride north. He will further instruct me in the ways of the Apache."

Her father had been eating silently until he could no longer remain silent. "Well, I'll be!" he said. "You'd go off traipsing around with that Indian? I should have shot him while I had the chance."

"Father, I expected more from you! You found me as a child. I was an Apache. Despite the many years, I still am the same. I can't make that change. All the years I was in Ireland I hungered for one thing. Foremost, sure I missed you, father, but the thing that I missed the most was to see the crimson red of a cactus flower in full bloom, to partake of its beauty. Something so foreign to this desert, yet such a part of it. I am part of this land, too. It calls out to me; I must answer.

"I will not be here when you return," her husband stated as he stood up and turned his back to her.

"What will you do?" she asked.

"I will return to Ireland where I belong. I will take our child with me."

With this revelation, Wink was visibly hurt. "It will only be for a short season," she said sadly.

Her father cleared his throat as if to get his daughter's attention. "What is the matter with you, child? Must you tear your life apart at its roots?"

"I will do no such thing, Father, you will see." With this she left the room.

Wink wanted to be on her horse before daylight. She wanted no further confrontations with her husband and father. She lingered over her sleeping baby, weeping on the outside, yet rejoicing on the inside for the chance to ride in quest for her beginnings. She blew the lamp out and kissed her son and left the room. Quintero was waiting for her on the trail to Apache Canyon. A simple greeting was exchanged on the move. They headed north to Metate Mound.

"This is one of the main camps of our people," Quintero said as they arrived at their destination. "They came here each harvest season to gather acorns and other necessities to prepare for winter. Do you remember being here as a child?

Wink shrugged her shoulders, gesturing uncertainly.

"Perhaps you will in time. We will stay here until I can contact Steve Ivory."

That night, as the fire burned, Quintero explained further to Wink the reason he would be taking Steve Ivory to the gold mine at Grasshopper Ridge. He also explained to her that he was a "keeper of the secrets," how his grandfather, Quintero, before him was the same. Before his father's death, he kept the secrets as well.

Quintero continued: "Before we ride, you must say that you are willing to do the same, that you are willing to die before you reveal what you know about the sealed mines I might show you."

Quintero quietly left the woman by the fire and went to the stone worn smooth by others. He sprinkled cornmeal and sat down. He began to sing to the bygone spirits who once were as he, a man fighting an uphill battle, to the creator for strength to carry out what he must do.

When Wink woke up, she was cold. The fire had burned to embers. She no longer heard the peaceful songs Quintero sang. Instead, she heard footsteps. She turned in the direction they came from in time to see Quintero about to spread a blanket over her. She smiled and wrapped the blanket tightly around herself and went back to sleep. Quintero put a few more small pieces of wood on the fire, then curled up in a blanket as well; he soon joined the woman in sleep.

The sun's appearance drove the sleep from the pair's eyes. Quintero told Wink he would ride to Willcox and find Steve Ivory. He asked her to stay at Metate Mound while he was gone. He encouraged her to use this time to seek her purpose to be here on Mother Earth. He would try to return in two days.

Wink had never been alone like this before. She fought with herself as the shadows began to form. Soon it would be dark. She had tried to convince herself all day long that she could handle it. Now, as realization struck, her fear tried to overcome her. She had fasted all day, trying to feel her inner strength. Quintero had left her a small bag containing sacred meal from the corn. She sprinkled it as she had been instructed. Next, she tried to get comfortable on the cold stone seat Quintero had called the "seat of the ancient ones." Her mind called out in prayer seeking audience with the greater powers; long into the night this continued. Morning found a cold, sleeping and collapsed woman on the stone chair. She woke up and looked around. She was all right, still at Metate Mound. She felt a stir of accomplishment inside her. She had tamed some of her fear and endured the night.

As the sun was in its highest point of flight, Wink found a place in the nearby stream where she could bathe. The water was as ice and she could not enjoy it for long. Afterwards, she stretched out among some large boulders and sunned herself. The heat radiating from the rocks felt good to her.

As darkness once more returned to the land, Wink fought again with her weaknesses. Pangs of hunger stung at her insides. Fear tried to conquer again; not content at the previous night's defeat, it battled on. Wink once more found the stone seat and sat down. She focused her thoughts on her childhood, the parts she could remember, and asked the Creator for an understanding. She always yearned to know how she came to be raised by the Irishmen instead of her people. Her head slumped. Startled she raised it and thought she had fallen asleep. When she opened her eyes, she saw people all around her in a circle. She rubbed her eyes for a second. Then opened them again--they were still there. A feeling of contentment filled her. Her head once more leaned forward. She entered the world of dreams.

The sun's blinding light probed at her until she could not put it off any longer, she opened her eyes. She was surprised to see she was still at Metate Mound. So real were her dreams the night before, she believed she had moved on to another place, a place where old and new co-existed. "How else could it be?" she reasoned. Her hand went to her face to brush the hair out of her eyes. She felt something moist on her skin. Pulling her hand away, she noticed the pigment of white paint. She went to her bags and found a small mirror she had hidden away for safekeeping. Looking at herself, she saw several white lines drawn upon her forehead. Cornmeal was in her hair as well. Gradually, the thoughts began to return-- the visitors from the night, the dreams, the dreamer.

Contentment filled her. She did not know everything she had questions of, yet she now knew she came from somewhere, from something very powerful and important, her beginnings. She had taken the oath to become a "keeper of the secrets."

Quintero still had not returned on the third day. Wink ate food for the first time since his departure. She walked the surrounding hills exploring, enjoying life. In a large boulder standing taller than the rest, were five metates worn deep into the stone. She pondered them for a moment, picturing herself watching women at work grinding away, talking and enjoying each other's company. Suddenly, a remembrance came to her of a child, in the shade of a nearby oak tree, watching the progress of the women. It was her, she now could place herself being here before. As she looked around she remembered other things, mostly unimportant, yet now she belonged.

The Irishman knew pain. He also was familiar with sorrow. He experienced both in his youth. What he felt now was an ache, something unfamiliar to him. He ached for the return of his daughter. Her husband and child had gone back to Ireland. He had taken them to board the train the day before. Now his home was quiet. The laughter once common to these walls was gone, replaced by the emptiness he felt. His wife tried as best she could to soothe his feelings, yet the weight remained heavy on his shoulders.

Quintero left his horse in the livery stable. He asked the man there how to locate the cowboy named Steve Ivory. He was obliging and pointed out directions to his house; it was but a short distance. The door opened as he drew close. A young boy came running past him on his way to the street.

"Is your Pa here?" Quintero asked.

"Yes, he's inside!" the boy said as he passed.

Quintero walked closer to the door and spoke. "Steve Ivory, are you in this house?" The dogs barked as they came running to the unfamiliar voice.

"Quintero!" Steve Ivory spoke as he saw the Indian. "Your arm is well?"

"Yes, it is well, strong as before," Quintero returned. "I came here as I said I would. Let's ride for Grasshopper Saddle," Quintero teased. Then a more serious tone came to his voice. "Have you the golden cross?"

"Yes, I have it!" Steve Ivory replied.

"Good, then we trade soon," Quintero said matter of factly.

"Not so fast," Steve Ivory replied; "just what do you propose?"

The Indian, in thought, paused for a moment. Then, looking directly into Steve's eyes, he replied, "I will give you two pack animals of gold. All the gold they can carry from the mine one time."

"How do I know you will fulfill your promise?" asked Steve.

"We will go to the mine first. When we return with the gold, you will give me the cross. Then our business will be over. Meet me tomorrow at the west end of Stockton Pass. From there we will ride to the gold mines." Quintero turned and left for the stables. He retrieved his horse and rode for Metate Mound.

It had taken much longer than it should have. Soldiers were on the move and he had to make his way around them without being seen. He had almost run into a small group of them as he passed the road to the Irishman's ranch. They were looking for him.

Wink was happy at his return. Quintero had considered that she might grow restless at his prolonged journey and actually return to her former life. He became more convinced of her desire to learn now that she had stayed in his absence.

"Tell me," he said, "have you discovered the way of the Apache?"

She looked away and said, "I am learning much."

Wink offered him food. He ate, then together they watched the sun depart. A small fire felt good to the two friends as the evening chill spread across the valley.

Silence prevailed most of the evening, and then Quintero spoke. "We will meet Steve Ivory tomorrow, then we head north. I am counting on you to help make this work," he said to the woman.

"I am ready!" she replied.

Quintero rolled out his bed and lay down. He was soon asleep. The woman stared into the fire in thought. As the hour grew late, she too made a bed and sought sleep.

The next morning Quintero caught their horses and led them into camp. Then he began to speak. "The only way we can get Steve Ivory to the mine without giving away the location is for everything to work out perfectly. If he becomes aware of the whereabouts of the mine, we will have to kill him. That is how important it is, to pull this off without a hitch. Since he is the only one to connect us to the cross, it is very important to me that we succeed."

Wink listened carefully as she packed her things.

"Soon as we meet Steve Ivory, we will ride," Quintero said. "We must put some distance between us and the soldiers at Ft. Grant. You will ride behind, watching to see if anyone follows. Steve Ivory might have told others of our agreement. We can't chance this happening. I will lead the way and keep an eye on Steve Ivory. If you see anyone or anything out of the ordinary, you are to ride hard to catch up and alert me."

Quintero then retrieved a leather belt from his bags. He took one of his knives from his own belt and stretched the new belt through it. He handed it to Wink. "Put this on," he said. "You might need it."

She hesitated for a moment, then did as he said. She smiled as she ran her hands around the belt. One of her hands came to rest on the knife. She felt its bone handle and nodded her head approvingly.

The horses were loaded with their belongings. Without speaking further, they mounted up and headed east.

Steve Ivory was waiting for them. His horse and two mules were grazing beyond the oak tree he was sitting under. "Beginning to wonder if I had the right day," he said.

"We came along as best we could," Quintero returned.

Steve Ivory tipped his hat and said, "Ma'am." to Wink. "Didn't know you were bringing the missus," he said looking towards Quintero.

"This is Wink. She is not my wife, but a good friend."

"My pleasure, Miss Wink. My name is Steve Ivory."

"How do you do, Mr. Ivory?" Wink said.

"You speak darn good English, ma'am," Steve Ivory returned.

Steve Ivory caught his animals and saddled them and was ready to ride in short order.

Quintero and Wink rested while he was making ready.

They proceeded through Stockton Pass and circled around the east end of Mt. Graham. Setting a course northeasterly, the riders headed to the Gila River, following it east to the San Francisco River.

The San Francisco River was one of the cradles of Apacheria. Here, year around water flowed, enough water to grow crops of pumpkin and maize. Deep canyons, stretching from the confluence of the Gila River to the box canyons of the borderlands of New Mexico, provided a natural roadway allowing commerce between various peoples of this part of the Southwest. It is said that Geronimo was born here. Most likely, it is so, for this was a fertile oasis in the broad deserts of the Southwest.

This land was the destination of the three horsemen. The Blue River empties into the San Francisco River, forming a small delta. The Membres people lived here, before the Apache, upon a ridge overlooking the small delta; a ruin attests to this. The Apache came to this country upon the wake of their departure. Their roots reached to the center of the earth-laying claim to this land as theirs.

Wink could feel the spirit of her people. She waited long into the day and rode hard into the night catching up to Quintero and Steve Ivory. She had ample time to ponder the greatness of those who were before her, the same who walked the very land she now traveled.

Evening found them camped upon the riverbank. The smell of mesquite wood burning filled the air. The sycamore trees and water mixed with the smoke added an earthly aroma to the canyon. Wink sought seclusion in the willows to bathe. She was bending over washing her hair when she first noticed the outline of a man sitting on rocks above her. She paused for a moment; long enough to see it was Quintero. He began to sing a song of the Apache. She turned her back to the man. It was then that she noticed the sun was setting in the sky to the west. She would give him the benefit of the doubt that the red glow of the setting sun was what held his attention. She finished her bath and walked back to camp in the darkness.

Steve Ivory was by the fire when she arrived. He saw the woman coming and stood out of habit to acknowledge her arrival. "Ma'am," he said as she drew closer. Wink smiled at the cowboy.

"You are a remarkable person," Steve said as she sat down.

"What do you mean?" Wink asked.

"You look like an Indian, yet you act and speak as a White."

"You are very observant," Wink spoke softly. "It is true. I am caught between both worlds. I was born as an Apache, yet spent my life with the Whites."

"What are you doing here then with Quintero?" Steve asked.

"I have spent a lifetime away from my people; yet in my absence they call out to me, bidding me to return and learn about my beginnings," Wink finished.

"Well, I wish you luck, ma'am," Steve offered. "You seem like a special lady to me."

Wink turned to face the fire. The flames dancing to the heat of the burning wood held her attention. She was still held captive when Quintero returned to camp.

Neither Steve Ivory or Wink acknowledged his arrival; both were pre-occupied by their own thoughts. Quintero found his blanket and stretched out on it. In time his eyes closed.

The horsemen took to the rim tops to escape the narrow bottomlands of the river. Quintero paused for a moment, stretched his arms and pointed at the fertile land below them. "In my Grandfather's time, our people farmed here.

A trail worn deep followed above, making travel easier than fighting the brush and quicksand below. Wink seldom traveled with the men. She took her job seriously and followed behind, watching, guarding the rear.

"Today, you will start wearing this," Quintero said as he produced an old flour sack and tossed it to Steve Ivory. It had a hole cut in it where his mouth would be, also a small hole for each ear.

"What is this for?" Steve asked.

"For your safety!" Quintero answered.

"What do you mean?" Steve asked.

"As long as you wear this, the location of the mine will remain secret and your life will be safe. Do not attempt to remove this sack during daylight hours. Otherwise, we cannot continue," Quintero finished.

Steve Ivory thought for a moment while rolling the sack with his hands. "O.K.!" he said.

"One other thing," Quintero added, "you ride here on in with your cinch loose as I fasten it."

"What the hell for!" Steve said loudly.

"That's just how it's done the last few miles," Quintero returned.

Steve Ivory keyed in on the Indian's final words; "the last few miles" kept rolling around in his memory. Excitement filled his dreams and he kept waking up, thinking it was time to face the day.

Wink met Quintero by the horses the following morning. "Why do you do these things, my brother?" she asked.

"He will be busy trying to keep balanced in his saddle, much to busy to second guess where we are. We will enter the area where he punches cattle. I must take this precaution so he doesn't figure out where he is."

Wink went to her horse and held it back as the two men rode north. She would wait beside the trail awhile before she followed them.

At the beginning of the journey, Wink felt pangs of disappointment. Yet, as time passed, she began to see that the solitude of this stark land was the greatest teacher of all. As the days passed, she found that the time she spent waiting was her school. Her thoughts came and went; each one sorted and reasoned away, to be stored until needed. Each passing day made her appreciate the simpler things, the things of the Indian way, the way of the Apache.

"We will reach the mines tomorrow," Quintero said in a hushed tone. "Do not say anything to Steve Ivory," he cautioned. "He must not be given things to map a route to the mine at a later time. Once there, we will rest while Steve Ivory collects his gold."

Wink listened as Quintero planned out the following day. She watched as her friend moved his arms back and forth showing how Steve Ivory rode his horse with the loose cinch. She seldom saw him laugh like he was doing. She looked beyond the fire and could see Steve Ivory had turned in early. He had a rough day riding. She, too, laughed along with Quintero.

TROUBLE ON THE HORIZON
Chapter 18

It had become common knowledge that Steve Ivory knew something about lost gold. Rumors had surfaced for a great while, linking it to him. The Uncle of Hector Antonne returned to Mexico a broken man, and it was only a matter of time until the tongue wagers let the rumors fall on Steve's shoulders. Many thought it was him who prevented them from finding the golden riches for themselves. Eyes followed him here and there; masked by various reasons, but just the same they were always watching.

The final gunfight in the wash at Dos Cabezas reinforced this feeling of resentment. Now, not only was Steve Ivory linked to the golden cross, but he and the renegade Apache had killed several of the local miners. Trouble was brewing in the mining camp and it was a deadly concoction of greed, hate and revenge.

Quintero noticed the man as he rode into the livery stable at Willcox, Arizona Territory. Something about his horse caught his eye. The man, however, had the kind of face that belonged to a thousand men. A beard hid the man's features leaving only eyes to reveal his identity. He had searching eyes, that is all Quintero could make of them. Quintero gave the bearded man the once over a last time, then walked over to the stable hand to ask directions to Steve Ivory's home.

The stranger brushed at his horse, then exited after Quintero did. From the alley behind the stable the stranger found the shade of the buildings. Here he could watch the Indian as he headed the short distance to his destination. While Quintero and Steve Ivory talked, the stranger cut through the alley and crossed the street, going into a saloon on Railroad Avenue. There, at the end of the bar, were two men he knew. After gulping down a whiskey he spoke in an excited voice telling them what he had just witnessed. One more quick shot of liquor and the three walked out together. The sunlight tore at their eyes, as they stepped into the street. The stranger nodded in the direction of the stable and the two friends followed along.

Two of the men saddled up and rode to the end of town and waited. The third man returned to the shadows of the alley and watched for Quintero's return.

After bidding Steve Ivory farewell, Quintero headed back to the livery stable. He paid little attention to the white man as he entered the stable and saddled his horse. The man fussed with his horse's feet, checking them as Quintero passed and entered the street. The horse Quintero thought he had seen somewhere before, was now gone he noticed. Mounting the stallion, he edged him north towards Metate Mound.

The tracks were easy enough to follow. The three men stayed back avoiding detection from keen eyes. The Indian, normally cautious, was detracted by a detachment of soldiers from Ft. Grant he encountered. Trying to avoid them put him in the position of one in flight, as he put many miles between them and him in short order. The three men following used this to their advantage and held his trail.

These three men came to Willcox to buy supplies. Two of them left Dos Cabezas earlier than the other. They finished buying what they needed and headed over to the saloon to wait on their friend. A night of whiskey and cards awaited them. That is, until the Indian rode into town. He changed it all. Now something more important waited on them. Gold was always more important! Yes, the drink and gambling could wait.

"Where do you think he's headed?" the one with the beard spoke quietly to his friends.

"Maybe the reservation," the closest friend returned.

"You sure he is the one?" the third man inquired.

"He's the one alright, saw him well. He went to the house of Steve Ivory, that cinches it in my book."

The three rode on in silence gaining a little distance on the Indian. They saw him enter a stand of oaks at the base of the mountain; he didn't ride out the other side. They pulled up in some brush and waited a safe distance from where they last saw Quitero.

The night was dark. The moon would not rise until later. When the sun's last reflections vanished from the mountain peaks, one of the strangers, on foot, narrowed the distance between the two camps, then crawled within sight of the Indian's camp at Metate Mound. He could see Quintero sitting on a rock, singing a chant unfamiliar to a man from the White's world. In the shadows of the campfire he saw the outline of a second person. Seeing enough, he carefully retreated to the safety of the darkness.

"Two of em," he told the others when he returned to his camp. "Didn't appear to be riled up any."

"Just the same," a voice came back from the darkness, "we better keep watch tonight."

The three men took turns posting a guard through the night. Morning found them ready to move on at the first sign of the Indians breaking camp.

Quintero left the oak grove first, followed by the second rider. They headed east skirting around Ft. Grant, headed towards Stockton Pass.

The three followers held back, riding along at a cautious pace. Reading the tracks of the horses for signs, no hurry was needed; they could tell plenty from them. One horseman, then the other, would take the lead. Two of the men would pause for awhile, then catch up to the first man. Taking turns this way; they did not draw attention to themselves.

At Stockton's Pass, the man in the lead pulled up fast and retreated into the trees and beat a quick back trail to the waiting two friends.

"The Indian's hooked up with Steve Ivory. He's drag'n two mules along with him," he said to the waiting men.

"What do you think they are up to?" one returned.

"I don't know, but I aim to see."

The three men stayed into the brush that was so abundant in the canyon bottom. When they heard the metal shoes of the horses striking rocks ahead, they likewise proceeded.

Upon crossing over the pass between the mountain and the Devil's Backbone, the shrubs became sparse until almost nonexistent. Here the grasslands of the San Simon Valley begin, at times mixed intermittently with mesquite trees and the like common to the Sonoran Desert. Tracking a man through a place like this could get a guy killed. One's eyes became so bold as if to cry out that they are the only senses required, placing the other four on edge. Herein lies the trouble; while one feels secure watching ahead, knowing he can see well and feels comfortable with the situation, sometimes allows the hunter to become the hunted.

"Let's hold up a minute," one of the men said to the others. "Looks like they let their horses blow here. Let's not crowd them."

One man held the horse's reins while the other two walked a short distance and relieved themselves. One of them produced some papers and soon the three had small cigarettes burning between their lips.

As the last puff of smoke left their lungs, the horsemen continued to trail their prey.

The grassland soon yielded to the lush vegetation of the river bottoms. They followed along easterly to the mountain country of the San Francisco River. Here the trail divided; one continuing into New Mexico, the other, up the Blue, and beyond. It was up the second trail they headed.

By now, the three men following them were aware that Wink was the rear scout, and a woman. They had watched her many times from the shadows as any predator would. They had seen her retreat to the bushes for privacy, tending to her natural needs.

"A woman," one said.

"She's a pretty thing," one of the men told the others as they watched her.

"Right nice looking Squaw," another agreed.

That night the pace quickened. Maybe it was the age-old lust of a man for a woman. "After all, she's a Squaw," they agreed. Selfish desire consumed better judgment as the men conspired amongst themselves. They figured tomorrow would be the day they would capture the woman.

Morning found them lying in wait for her. They knew she would hold back and let the two men ride on ahead of her. It would give them the time they needed to carry out their dastardly plan.

"What the hell!" one of the men said under his breath.

"That Indian is plain loco," the other man returned.

"I think he is going to hang the S.O.B.; why else the hood over his head?"

They stared in disbelief as Quintero led the horse along that was carrying Steve Ivory.

The woman retreated, for the moment, into the back of the minds of the three desperadoes.

When Wink moved forward, the men cautiously followed behind.

The afternoon sun was warm, and felt good as Wink sat with her back resting against a smooth rock. She watched the trail wind its way below her. They had traveled it earlier in the day. Now, she alone enjoyed the peacefulness of this place, unaware of the danger lurking at her heels. Her eyes grew heavy, so she stretched out on the rock, enjoying its warmth, her eyes closed.

From a vantage point beyond her, a pair of wanton eyes watched her every move, eyes that knew she was asleep. They drew closer; just a quick look they figured, that is all.

Wink stirred, shifting her position as the hard bed she lay upon ate at her back. Rolling over on her side, she now positioned her face away from the man whose eyes watched.

Becoming bolder, he drew closer than he should have. Freezing in mid step, as a twig snapped under his boot. The noise sounded as a gunshot to his ears. He stared at the woman to see if she heard. She continued sleeping as before, unaware of her current danger. Her horse pulled at its reins, breaking the small branch it was tied to. She raised her head and looked around, seeking the source of annoyance to the horse. The ears of the woman's horse were raised, and it was facing the stranger. Looking at the horse first, then turning to see what had startled it, she saw the outline of a man.

He knew he had been spotted when he saw her bolt for her horse. The bush he tried to hide behind was to small for him, unable to conceal his bulkish body. He sprang at her, grabbing the horses reins as she tried to mount. Then, grabbing her hair, he pulled her away from the horse.

Wink's hand went to her knife; as the man pulled her to him, she turned and arched it towards him cutting his cheek, letting blood flow down his face. Anger burned in his eyes as he delivered a punch to her head. Wink's world went dark, as she folded into a pile onto the ground. She awoke to the man pouring water on her face. As her eyes opened, he pulled her to her feet; then, grabbing a handful of hair pulled her towards her horse. Then, grabbing the horse by its reins, he led them down the trail towards his friends.

"I caught her!" he said when he met up with the others.

The two men looked at each other in disbelief.

"Thought we were going to wait," one said.

"She saw me. I had to stop her from telling the others," he returned.

Wink listened as the three men spoke of her as an object without an identity, something to own, with no concern of consent. For the first time since this ordeal began, Wink was scared. The feeling crept up her back raising small bumps in its wake. She was all too aware of the three pairs of eyes prying into her secret places.

The men led her into a stand of oak, off the trail, and tied her to a sturdy branch of one of the trees. Then they moved away from her and conversed amongst themselves.

The sun would soon end its flight. Behind it, the blackness that hides all things would arrive. Once more, the cold crept up the woman's back and arms. She wished to cry out in pain, but she would not. She had not made a sound since this ordeal began. Nor would she give them the satisfaction of hearing her cry out. She was Apache.

Wink's knife had cut deeply into her attacker's cheek. Blood still issued from the wound. When the three men returned to camp, one of them dug through his principles and produced a needle and some thread. He skillfully stitched up the wound, as the injured man cursed madly at the woman. When the task was complete, he walked over and backhanded her across the face, once more putting her to the ground. Both eyes were now swollen, rendering her almost blind. She shivered as the cold returned.

"It was not like Wink to stay behind for such a long time," Quintero thought as the evening darkened. Steve Ivory and himself had long since turned their animals to graze; still Wink was absent. He watched from a large boulder, searching the darkness for any sign of her return; finally it was useless to try to see any further.

"What do you suppose is keeping her?" Steve asked.

Quintero remained silent, hiding his worry as best he could.

The Indian kept the fire going for his friend, anticipating her return at any minute. It occupied his time, allowing his mind a distraction from worry.

The sun arrived, still no trace of Wink. Quintero shook Steve Ivory, pulling him from sleep. As his eyes opened, and looked around, he could see the woman had not returned. Then his eyes widened in disbelief at the gun aimed between them.

"What's this about" Steve demanded.

"Hate to do this to you, but I can't let you loose without the sack over your head." Quintero returned.

"That's crazy!" Steve said loudly. "Wink needs my help too. What are you aiming on doing, kill me?"

Quintero pushed the rifle into Steve's ribs and prodded him towards a nearby tree.

"Back up and put your hands behind your back! I don't have anymore time."

The horses were nearby. Quintero caught his and tied Steve's animals so they wouldn't follow him.

"Don't be a fool!" Steve yelled, as Quintero rode away.

Quintero could see the place ahead where he had last seen Wink. He tied his horse in some trees and proceeded ahead on foot. Something bothered him about this place; he sensed trouble.

They had seen no one since this journey began. Staying to themselves and not following the more popular routes had made this possible. Yet, now something was wrong. His hand brushed his knife at his side. A quick motion brought his rifle to his hands, in the ready position. Carefully he picked his way along the trail.

The sun reflecting from the blade of the knife that he had given Wink, was not a good omen. Quintero bent over and collected it. He ran his finger through the blood on its blade, all the while not taking his eyes from the trail beyond him. Like a cat, he continued, senses keen to the slightest change.

They knew he would come; someone would return for the woman. They waited like a tick after a feeding. Stuck tight, waiting in the shade of the trees, a trap was set. Wink, still tied to the tree, was the bait. Yes, all they had to do was wait.

Wink could not see her attackers, but she heard plenty. She knew of the extreme danger she now faced. She felt sorrow that she had placed Quintero and Steve into this. She blamed herself for taking a nap, instead of watching the trail.

Quintero followed the tracks of Wink and another. He could tell the new tracks were of a large man wearing boots. The heels dug into the earth as he walked. He could see that Wink had struggled with her attacker, yet it was obvious the man had prevailed.

Now he, Quintero, blamed himself for putting her in danger. His own desire for this beautiful woman had clouded his mind and prevented him from using good judgment. Now it all came down upon him with crushing force.

The tracks left the trail and entered a thicket of oaks. Here, the tracks were joined by two other men. The hammer on the rifle sounded as thunder as he pulled it back. "Only Usen, the Great Spirit, controlled his fate now," he thought as he paused by the edge of the trees. His eyes searched into the darkness of the shaded grove, trying to penetrate its interior. Carefully he entered into the unknown. A loud thump rained upon his head. His rifle discharged as it fell from his hands, and the report echoed up the canyon. Quintero lay in a state of unconsciousness upon the moist ground.

Steve Ivory struggled with the rope that bound his hands behind his back. He cussed the Indian for leaving him tied up, unable to help find Wink. The knots finally yielded to him as the sound of gunfire reverberated through the canyon. He strapped on his six-gun and headed towards his horse. Halfway, it occurred to him that they were probably dealing with outlaws who, most likely, would kill him if he wasn't careful. No, he would not discount the dangerous aspect of it, but instead reasoned that perhaps taking the offensive might be the best chance they had for getting out of this mess alive.

Most likely, someone caught Wink off guard, desperados who would stop at nothing to have their way, probably had been following them for sometime. Maybe they might figure him to be a prisoner, when he didn't return with the Indian. He rubbed his chin for a minute, then went about his plan.

Taking his spare clothes from his saddlebag, he filled them with dried grass until, from a distance, it looked like a man. He positioned it against the tree where Quintero had left him tied. Placing his hat on top finished it.

Steve found a place behind a rock where he could watch the trail to their camp. He grew impatient as the day passed. Then, from the corner of his eye, he caught movement. Focusing his attention, he saw it was indeed a large man sneaking towards their camp. While pausing, this man signaled up the ridge to a second man. It took awhile to find the second man, as he was concealed, like himself, behind a boulder. If he let the attackers get to close, they would know the man they were watching was only a sham. It was a long chance, but the only one he had. The hammer on the rifle pulled back with ease, to the ready, like him.

The man below him was circling, inching closer towards camp. Above him the second man watched the progress of the lower man. Steve made up his mind he would hold his fire until the lower man reached camp, or showed any change in actions. The hardest part was the waiting and wondering about his Indian friends.

Below him, the man paused for a moment, then tossed a small pebble. Sensing something out of place, he turned around and headed back the way he came, pausing once more to signal his friend on the hill. At this moment, Steve gently pulled the trigger. The man on the ridge was dead before the sound of the rifle, doing its work, found his ears. The next shot, like the first, did its job as well. The man below him joined the first, over there, somewhere.

Steve watched, and listened, searching for anything out of place. It was not long before the sound of steel striking stone reached his ears. As the rider approached, Steve lowered himself behind the rock, as before. The rider appeared below him, working his way along on the trail. Behind, on foot, were Quintero and Wink. Their hands, bound together at the end of ropes, allowed them to be pulled along by the rider.

"That's it," Steve whispered. "Come a little bit closer."

The rider came to a halt. Steve once more pulled back the gun's hammer. He heard the man call, "Tad, you there?" then again, "Zeb, where you at?"

Steve quietly, under his breath, once more called for him to come in a little closer. All the while he kept his aim. Shortly, the rider tugged on his captives' rope and kicked his horse in its flanks. He was making for some cover ahead. Steve knew before the bullet left his gun that his aim was bad. It crashed into a rock below the horse's feet. Fragments of stone pelted the animal, spooking it, causing it to rear up onto its hind legs. Quintero and Wink pulled the horse over backwards onto the rider. It had been a mistake tying the ropes to his saddle horn.

They pounded on the man with a rock, finishing him off. Quintero stood by as Wink drove the last breath from the man. Wink saw her knife in the dead man's belt. She stood up and reached for it. After cutting the rope, that bound their hands, she returned to the dead man. She stood over him, passing the knife over the dead man's head several times; then broke into a chant. Apache words flowed from her tongue. Quintero looked on as Wink performed a ceremony of times past, a time of greatness, a time of the Apache. He wondered silently where these words came from, put in the mouth of a woman who was raised by the Whites, no longer speaking her native tongue; yet, this day she spoke flawless Apache. "She has found her beginnings," he reasoned. Blood ran down her arms as she raised the lifted scalp for all to see. A shrill echo reverberated up the narrow canyon, a shadow crossed in front of the Indians, Steve Ivory looked skyward, a giant eagle circled above. Once more the scream of the eagle could be heard, sounding its approval of the happenings below.

Wink collapsed against Quintero. Steve could tell she was sobbing by the jerking movement of her body. Yet, he heard nothing.

Steve helped them towards camp. Wink's eyes were swollen from the beating she suffered, and Quintero had a wound on his head, where he had been pistol-whipped. They did not refuse his help.

After Quintero had rested, he said to Steve: "We are even, my friend."

"What do you mean?" Steve inquired.

"I saved you at Dos Cabezas. Now you saved me here, we are even."

Steve Ivory caught his horse and rode down the trail. Rounding up the other five horses, he returned to camp.

Upon seeing the gray horse again, Quintero recalled the day in the livery stable in Willcox. He knew this horse was the same one he saw there. Then it came to him. It was also the horse he had turned loose upon the ridge above Hector's grave.

"Tomorrow, we will begin our journey anew. The gold mines are close now. We will tie the dead men upon their horses and take them with us. Their disappearance, like the gold itself, will become part of the mystery known only to a few, understood by even fewer." finished Quintero.

They would release the three men's horses when the grizzly task was completed, allowing them to become part of a band of wild horses that frequented the canyon where the mines were located.

Wink and Quintero never spoke again of the events that transpired that night. He endured the pain of seeing the woman he loved used by the three outlaws. If Wink hadn't scalped her attacker, Quintero would have skinned him alive. A punishment he felt more appropriate.

Wink became with child, as the result of that encounter, and named the boy child "Jack." He was a mixture of the three men's juices. Later many would refer to him as "Crazy Jack," a name of which at times was not unfounded.

Wink loved Jack, but was torn between that love and the memory of the hated night from which he sprang. It was a battle that raged inside of her the rest of her life.

THE SHADOW OF TRUTH
Chapter 19

Steve Ivory was having a hard time staying aboard his horse with the loose cinch. The trail was steep, with many switchbacks. He had lost all sense of direction, since the hood had been placed over his head. All he had was the assurance from the Indian that they would reach their destination this day.

From her vantage point, Wink could see the two men winding up the opposite side of the canyon. A hawk screamed below her and caught an updraft; it soared higher and higher. She could hardly see it now as she strained her eyes. Once more, her attention focused on the two men. They no longer were in view. This surprised her. She expected them to continue up the hillside. After watching for a couple more hours and no further sight of them, she mounted her horse and gave it its lead. The horse was anxious to catch up to the others.

Steve Ivory could smell water, it was apparent the animals could also, they had a sense of urgency to their step. They were headed down hill now and the going was easier. Quintero jerked the lead-rope on Steve Ivory's horse bringing it to a halt.

"You can remove the hood now!" said Quintero.

"About time!" Steve Ivory returned.

"We are almost there," Quintero spoke. "Around the bend is a flat spot. We will camp there."

Steve Ivory looked around; the canyon was narrow and shaded. Steep rocky bluffs towered above them, blocking the afternoon sun. After tightening the cinch on his horse, he removed the lead rope and tossed it to Quintero. A short ride found them at the place Quintero spoke of. A small pool of water below a rock cliff was opposite their campsite. Steve could see, in times past, that a sizeable waterfall kept the pool filled. Now a small trickle of water ran down the face of the cliffs. Steve ambled over and bent low to the ground; his canteen began to accept water. The pool was deeper than he thought it would be. The edges adjoining the cliffs were dark; indicating the water was even deeper there. It was while thus bent over, he noticed little nuggets of gold embedded into the rock floor extending from the pool. Most of them were about the size of a small match head. At first he couldn't believe what he saw. His hand found his knife. Prying with it, a small nugget came loose. His hand was shaking as he held it up to look at.

"Gold!" he said with a raspy voice. "Gold! Gold!" he laughed.

Quintero looked on from a distance, he had been busy setting up camp; now, his attention focused on Steve Ivory. The Indian shook his head in wonderment at the white man. "Gold always makes them crazy," he thought to himself.

Wink found where their tracks passed through a narrow rock gate leading into another canyon. She followed, entering into a canyon not visible to the eye from a distance. Large trees lined the creek bottom, further shading the little oasis. Turning around a small hill, she saw the horses and mules grazing ahead. She pulled up beside Quintero and dismounted.

"Steve has already found gold," Quintero offered, as they walked towards the pool of water.

Wink walked over to where Steve Ivory was panning. He looked up and smiled at her, raising the pan so she could see the small bits of color in the bottom of it.

"My goodness!" Wink said at the sight of the gold.

Steve went back to working his pan until only the gold remained. Shovel full after shovel full of gravel was retrieved from the bottom of the pool, each going into the pan to be separated. A respectable amount of gold was retrieved before it became too dark to see. The gold was placed in a small pile on a pie tin to dry. One larger sized nugget to the side of the pile was equal to about one third of the dust. Steve focused his attention on it. "Half as big as a chicken egg," he said, as he held it closer to the fire. The dull yellow glow became more brilliant as the flames played upon it. Quintero acknowledged the nugget Steve displayed, but it was obvious he was unimpressed

"You must not leave this canyon until we are ready to go out together!" Quintero warned. "When you are finished mining your two mule loads of gold, we will leave. Until then, you stay here by this stream. The gold follows it. There is plenty to keep you busy. Do you understand?" Quintero looked straight at Steve Ivory.

"Yes, I understand," he replied.

Quintero left camp as the darkness increased. It was but a short while until Wink and Steve Ivory heard the first of his singing. Then it grew louder echoing down the narrow, but deep canyon.

Wink did not hear Quintero return to camp. Her eyes grew heavy and sleep came upon her. Sometime in the night, she heard the call of a lonesome coyote. It sounded as if it came from here, then there, as the sounds bounced from the rocks. Soon another picked up the chorus and joined the first. She saw Quintero's outline in the darkness. He was rolled up in a blanket. Both men slept through the serenade.

Wink's thoughts journeyed from this place--to Ireland, to her son and husband. She summoned them back, but they would not obey. They were not content here with her in the land of her ancestors, but instead sought to trouble her with the present. She fought an inner battle plagued with guilt the rest of the night. No reasoning on her behalf was acceptable as her conscience found her guilty of offense. She was glad when the sun returned to warm her of the cold that tore at her insides.

Three winds blow down
The canyon called life.
The gentle breeze of youth quickly
Fades, pushed aside
As turbulence swells,
And all too soon wind erodes,
The innocence of the child.
To late to discover one is caught
Up in the whirlwinds of life.

    Quintero had led the mules past the entrance, trying to lay a false trail beyond their destination.

    Wink spent part of the day watching the trail where it entered the canyon. She surveyed the horizon, searching for any sign of movement. There was none, so she rode back to camp.

    Steve Ivory had amassed a large pile of gold in a short time. Unfortunately his back was giving out from the hard work. His enthusiasm never wavered; however, it just slowed him down somewhat. The afternoon found him wandering down the stream. Upon the bank, above the creek, he came to the ruins of a small cabin. The walls had long since decayed, but the fireplace and stone foundation remained. He nosed around, then retraced his steps back to camp.

    Quintero had fallen in behind, watching Steve Ivory. He could not let him leave the canyon and see landmarks that might enable him to return later, on his own. Yet he did not expose himself to the miner. He came into camp a few minutes after Steve Ivory did.

    "I am not the first white man to search for gold here. I saw the ruins of an old house down yonder," Steve said as he pointed his arm in the direction of the ruins.

    "Yes, others have came here before," Quintero said. "They mined gold. It is here, as you know, for the taking; yet their greed consumed them, turning to rage until it destroyed them. When I was young, bones littered this place where many men were killed. My grandfather said they killed each other over the yellow metal."

    Steve figured there was much more to it than this, yet he accepted the part of the many bones littering the cabin site. He figured some of Quintero's people killed the unlucky miners.

    Wink had used Steve Ivory's shovel and dug a hole to catch the small trickle of water. As it passed through a thicket of willows, there she would bathe. Try as she might, she could not shake off her worry from the previous night. It played at her through the day and promised to destroy her rest again this night. Quintero sensed something was weighing heavy on the woman's mind. He tried extra hard to spark her interest in what he was doing, yet she seemed uninterested. He finally decided she must need time alone to solve what was troubling her.

Steve Ivory had quit for the day. He was tired and found the shade refreshing as he napped.

Wink went to the stand of willows. Quintero could hear her pounding her clothes with rocks to clean them. This sound was followed by silence. Quintero busied himself around the fire. Soon the stew he was making would be done.

It grew dark and Wink had not returned. Quintero was concerned. His rifle was leaning against a fork in a small tree; picking it up, he headed towards the direction Wink had gone. He did not find her at the small pool she had dug. Continuing down the stream, at a large pile of boulders, he heard the sound of her weeping. A twig snapped making noise to announce he was close. Wink continued sobbing; she tried to suppress it as she saw him approach.

"What troubles you, sister?" asked Quintero.

"I am fighting a battle against sorrow," Wink returned.

Drawing closer, Quintero could see Wink was naked, her clothes hung in the bushes around her. He hesitated for a moment, and then Wink stood up and faced him.

"Hold me," she said reaching her arms to him.

"You are cold. Why are you not dressed?" Quintero asked.

"My clothes are still wet," the woman replied.

Quintero stepped towards the woman. She wrapped her arms around him and buried her head on his shoulder. Quintero's hand brushed one of her ample breasts as she reached for him. He felt her softness as she pressed herself against him. Pausing to focus on what he was doing, he held the woman tightly as she cried. His hands wrapped around her shoulders. When her crying stopped, he removed his shirt and placed it around her. He built a small fire and moved her clothes close to it. The woman in her natural state was the most beautiful sight he had beheld as the firelight bounced upon her skin. Quintero looked away; he could stand no more.

"What is the matter?" Wink asked. "Are my burdens to great for your shoulders to bear?"

"I have fought many men to the death, yet the hardest battle I have fought was the one here tonight with myself. I hunger for you more than anything I have ever wanted, yet a promise holds me bound."

"It pains me that I have troubled you. You are a great man," Wink said as her hand reached and found his. "Thank you," she said softly.

Quintero found her clothes with his free hand. "They are dry now," he said as he offered them to her.

Wink stood then stepped into her clothes.

It was with regret, and, yet, a feeling of accomplishment that he watched the clothed woman walk towards camp.

Steve Ivory was asleep when they returned. Several bags of gold were piled against a nearby tree. "About one mule load" Quintero figured. Tomorrow he would show Steve Ivory a place where the nuggets were bigger and more plentiful. The golden cross was waiting for him. He was anxious to posses it. Then all this would be over. Once more, his thoughts returned to Wink. "Would it be over?"

The following morning Quintero showed Steve Ivory a nugget bed further down the stream. Bedrock was shallow and the gravel adjoining it yielded much gold. Quintero then announced he was going to go hunting for some camp meat.

"Have luck!" Wink said, as he headed from camp.

Wink climbed up the hillside trying to watch Quintero as he hunted. She could see him riding the finger ravines sloping down from the rim tops above. It was a peaceful morning, easy to lose oneself in the simplicity of the moment.

A stone, rolling against another, alerted Wink to movement below her. She fixed her eyes in the direction the sound came from. Steve Ivory was disobeying and heading up the side of the mountain toward her. He must have figured she went with Quintero. Wink crawled the distance she was from the arroyo; Steve was headed up. She was concealed in the abundant grass, her heart pounded as the distance narrowed. She clutched her knife tightly and sprang to her feet knocking the man over backwards. Her knife drew blood as it cut his arm. Wink rolled on top of the stunned cowboy and held her knife to his throat. His eyes widened in disbelief as he stared at the knife blade and then into the eyes of the woman. Trying to reason what his chances were of living through this, Steve tried to speak, but all he could do was strain to fill his lungs. Falling against a large rock had knocked the wind from him.

Seeing his helplessness softened Wink, she stood up over him. And helped him gain his footing and together they headed back to camp.

"Why don't you join me?" Steve Ivory asked when his voice returned. "There's a fortune in gold in this place; enough for all of us to be rich."

"Hold your tongue! Must you behave as a fevered man? Two mules of gold will last you a lifetime, yet you put yourself at risk. Where are your wits?" Wink said sharply. "You try to climb to the ridge tops again and it will cost you your life."

Quintero returned to camp leading his horse. A large deer hung over its sides. The man's smile disappeared as he saw a bruised Steve Ivory by the fire. Blood still seeped through the bandage on his arm. Anger replaced the smile as he turned to the woman. "Did he make it to the ridge tops?"

"No, I stopped him," Wink replied.

"So he saw nothing?" Quintero once more asked.

"He saw nothing of importance. I stopped him before he could see any landmarks," she replied.

"You are a fool! Greed strips you of your senses," Quintero said as he looked at Steve Ivory. "I know where there are enough bags of gold hidden to finish off your load. We will get it tomorrow and be on our way."

The evening was spent caring for the meat Quintero had killed. This night they feasted upon the abundance of the land. Maybe tomorrow they would hunter.

Quintero slipped away from camp early the next morning. He returned mid day leading one of Steve Ivory's mules. It was straining under a heavy load. Upon reaching camp, Quintero led the mule close to Steve and handed him its lead rope.

"See if it meets with your approval," Quintero said.

Steve Ivory dumped one of the buckskin bags into his gold pan. Large nuggets fell out of the bag. It was of a better quality than what he had recovered.

"I will accept it," Steve Ivory said as he looked in Quintero's direction.

"Good! Then let's ride for home," Quintero returned.

Steve Ivory once more was required to wear the sack over his head. His cinch was also loosened as before. Quintero gathered pleasure in seeing him struggle to keep balance.

It took less time for them to reach the San Francisco River leading Steve to believe they returned by a different trail. The ride back to home was uneventful. Steve Ivory spoke little to the two Indians. He once more felt as if he had been outwitted by Quintero. Excitement that swelled inside of him was still hard to contain; yet, he dare not let it show. A day would shortly be at hand, however, when he could let it explode. Even though Quintero was one smart red man who was a challenge to out-fox, still two mules loaded with gold was no small feet in itself. He could live with it. He had no regrets.

Quintero hid the gold in a cave at Stockton Pass. He would wait there until Steve Ivory returned with the golden Cross of St. Stephen. If Steve Ivory did not return in three days he would bury it in a more secure place.

Wink took position higher up the mountain where she could see a long distance. She would alert Quintero if anyone approached. Quintero guarded the cave, just in case.

On the third day, Steve Ivory showed as planned. The cross was handed to Quintero, who held it towards the sun, then he looked at Wink; her smile met his.

"The gold is over here," Quintero said, as he walked towards the direction to which he pointed.

Steve Ivory offered his hand to the Indian. Quintero paused for a moment, then smiled and took his hand.

"I guess I don't blame you for trying," Quintero said as they shook hands.

Steve Ivory looked at Wink. "Ma'am," he said slowly, "you hold a mean knife. As fine a warrior as I ever went against," he finished as he turned away.

Quintero and Wink gathered their horses and rode for Metate Mound.

LIFE HAS MANY JOURNEYS
Chapter 20

"What will you do when this is finished?" Quintero asked.

"I long to see my baby, so I will return to Ireland. If I stay there will depend on my husband. The last time I saw him, he was angry. Just the same, my child calls out to me in the night." Wink finished.

"We all must do as our spirit directs," Quintero returned.

"What is yours telling you?" she inquired.

"I am still searching for answers," he said.

They continued in silence to Metate Mound. As evening faded, red outlined the Galiuro Mountains to the west. Quintero went to the stone of the ancient ones. He produced corn meal from a small bag, and sprinkled it on to the ground. After taking seat, his song filled the air. Wink sat by a small fire, grazing into its embers, letting the dancing flames and Quintero's singing soothe her thoughts.

Steve Ivory hid most of his gold on the way back to Willcox. "It would be foolish to bring in so much at once," he reasoned. Folks would kill him for it if they knew he had so much gold. Instead, it would be his bank account. It would be safe where he hid it until needed.

Quintero woke early. The sun was yet to show itself.

"Hurry, let's ride!" Quintero said to Wink as he shook her gently.

"What's wrong?" Wink wanted to know.

"Nothing is wrong," Quintero said. "I am anxious to once more be on the move, to feel alive as the earth changes when I pass."

The cross was carefully tied upon the back of a horse. It now resembled a pack frame with supplies strapped on top of it. They headed west, avoiding well-used trails, instead making their own way across the desert.

"How far will this journey lead us?"

"I have been instructed to place the cross in a certain cave. Then it will be over." Quintero replied. "It will take but a short while. Will you see it through with me?"

"Yes," Wink replied, then added, "Why have you been so silent?"

"I am heavy with sadness at the thought of losing one who lives here," Quintero said as his arm rested on his heart.

Wink crossed the few steps between them and kissed the man on his cheek.

"You must not!" Quintero replied. Yet his strength was not sufficient to push her away.

"I am weak, do not test me," he once again replied. He held her tightly, then released her.

As she slowly backed away, she looked at Quintero and replied, "I am weak as well."

"A river had to be crossed, then more desert," Quintero explained. "Yet, we are almost to our destination. This day we will finish the task."

"Why are we not happy then, my brother?" Wink replied.

"It is the uncertainty that we may never meet again," Quintero said.

"Yes, that sounds true," Wink replied. "We must let our spirits soar as the eagle while we are together. For tomorrow is another life. This day is all we share. We love, yet we must not love. Our spirits are drawn together by our beginnings, by our people and, yes, love. So let us take what pieces of happiness we find and fit them together into something that is good for us. I would like to see my brother happy, for it will put a smile in my heart to carry with me when I think of this time we have had."

A long ride brought them to a deep canyon. A spring supplied water to a small creek winding its way down the mountain until it spilled into the desert. The canyon spilt off a high mountain; as it cascaded downward, its color changed, making it a breath-taking picture. The two watched as the shadows grew longer, changing everything in its wake.

"Why do we wait?" Wink inquired.

"You will soon see," Quintero replied.

Impatience showed on Wink's face.

"It's almost time," spoke Quintero.

"The sun is almost gone and we have no camp," Wink returned.

"There!" Quintero said as he pointed his hand.

"What do you see?" Wink inquired.

"Over there, they grow to many," Quintero said, as he once more pointed them out.

"What?" Wink asked again.

"Bats, the cave we seek is there home, Quintero replied. "I have only been here one other time with my Grandfather. This is how we found it."

The torches Quintero made at Metate Mound were packed with the golden cross. He walked to his horse and retrieved them. He handed the golden cross to Wink as he lit the bunches of dry sage.

"Let's look at it one more time," Wink said. "I have never seen anything that compares with its beauty in all the Cathedrals in Ireland," she finished.

"Only one thing compares to its beauty," Quintero added, as his eyes focused on Wink; then pulling the buckskin bag around the cross he headed up the canyon.

The opening to the cave was small. They crawled inside on their stomachs. Once in, however, it opened up into a large tunnel. They walked farther into it and a cavern appeared. On one side was a stone shelf, upon which sat several rusty old chests. Many bars of gold were stacked by them. A larger stack of silver bars was in a long row beyond them.

"What's in the chests?" Wink asked.

"Let's look!" Quintero replied.

They walked closer to the stone bench. Quintero leaned forward and opened the largest box. As the light entered, the unmistakable glow of yellow metal shown from it. Goblets and candleholders made of gold were piled inside. Quintero laid the Cross of St. Stephen with the other objects and closed the lid. He opened a smaller chest next to the one they looked inside. It contained more of the same.

"I have seen enough," Wink said. "Let's leave this place."

They returned the way they came. It was dark when they reached their horses. They rode to the bottom of the canyon and made camp by the creek.

Quintero stopped by the fork in the road. One led to the Irishman's ranch and mine, the other one to Willcox.

He paused for a moment. "You are an Apache woman warrior," Quintero said softly. "You have drawn blood protecting the secret places. You will always be a keeper of the secrets. Ride proud," he finished. Then he turned his horse to ride away.

"Wait!" Wink called out.

Puzzled, Quintero turned his horse around.

"The Irish in me demands more than this," she said smiling.

They dismounted and embraced. "I will always remember you," she whispered in his ear.

"A day will not pass that I will not think of you," Quintero returned. He jumped on his horse and rode for Metate Mound.

The Irishman had long since gotten over his hurt. He rejoiced at seeing his stepdaughter again.

"Where have you been?" he inquired.

"I cannot say," she replied. "I am here now, that's all that matters. I will not be staying. I must go to my baby," she said to her father. "Will you return with me to Ireland so I can see him?"

"You hear that, dear?" he called to his wife.

"Yes, I did!" the woman replied. "Yes, we will go together."

The three stood embracing, feeling of each others love.

Quintero breathed deeply of the mountain air; the aroma of cedar filled his nostrils. It was good to be home. His family surrounded him, so much to talk about, so much to do.

"It is over," he thought. "The cross is safe." Then his mind wandered to the stone bear he placed on Wink's neck. "It is well," he thought; "his Grandfather would approve."

One day he would take his son to the cave and show him the golden cross. "He will be a keeper of the secrets," Quintero reasoned. "I will tell him the story of how it fell into our hands. And of Grandfather and Hector Antonne, the woman warrior, Wink. He would hold nothing back. And if the Antonnes should come again from Mexico to search for the cross, that day will be the day to decide…"

Many years later, the first car Steve Ivory had ever seen came rattling up the street in front of his house.

"Well, I'll be!" he said. "Have you ever?"

"That's an automobile, Father!"

"I know, son," he said; "never thought I'd live to see the day."

"Steve, would you knock off the tall tales and hurry. We are going to be late for the picnic," Mary yelled.

"O.k., o.k.," he muttered.

"What about the cross, Father?"

"I found it, all right. I followed a lucky bear track up a wash to it. Traded it to an Indian named Quintero, to take me to the Lucky Boy Mine. He let me mine all the gold two mules could carry."

"Is that why some people call you Lucky?"

"Well sorta, it's part of the story," Steve Ivory added.

"Will you guys hurry. It is starting as we speak!" Mary yelled.

"Well, we'll talk more later, boys. We'd better not keep your Mother waiting."

Quintero noticed the woman hanging the sandal over the doorway to their home. His time away had been long, and she hungered for his return. He knew her well, and her actions spoke loudly to him. Perhaps once more the sandal would lead the footprints of the unborn to his wiki-up, thereby granting her wish. It would please him as well.

Many horses waited in the surrounding pastures, they must be trained to ride and traded for supplies. They, like him, unruly in their ways, traced their roots to this land, Apache land.

Many seasons came and went, marking their passing with the fruit they bore. Two times his wife gave birth to sons. Each one, strong and well formed. Each one, reminding him of the goodness of life. Each one, filling the footsteps of them who passed before on a journey called life. He pondered these things many times late into the night, marveling at how it all came to be, and will yet be.

The changing times brought fewer men searching for gold. The secret places were watched over, but the vastness of the former lands of Apacheria denied him the satisfaction of stopping it altogether. He remained content with small victories here and there.

At times, the urge to feel the wind in his face found him. The stallion grew restless like him and needed its rein, he reasoned. It was these times that he would, once more, find himself at the old camps of his people, Metate Mound being his favorite. There he could feel his grandfather, and remember the times they shared. He found himself drawn to the Irishmen's mine once. The house was empty and he could tell only a caretaker remained keeping a vigil over it. His thoughts traveled to the distant land Wink spoke of, his heart filled with her memory and he hoped she was well.

The Whites, never content to be without victory, continued to find places to march. Word reached his ears from far off lands many times, telling him of battles fought and won in these places. Quintero could hardly understand how this could be. To fight for something other than food or to preserve your home was foreign to him.

One day, while tending his crop of corn, he heard the sound of Mexican cartwheel spurs jingling from the ridge tops above him, a sound familiar from his past. Stopping his work, he listened once more, searching for its source. Three men appeared, riding through the cedar trees. All were decked out in fine Mexican attire. He had seen clothes like this before on Señor Antonne; Steve Ivory had called him a dandy. Here before him rode three such men. Coming to a halt at the fence, surrounding his small plot of corn, they dismounted.

"We search for a man named Quintero," one of them spoke.

"I am he," said Quintero.

"Our grandfather has sent us on this quest, to search for the golden Cross of St. Stephen."

"And how is your grandfather?" Quintero asked as he studied the three young men.

"He has traveled to the land of the dead. Before his departure, he extracted an oath from us to make this journey to your land and seek out the cross that has brought my family so much misfortune, and return it to its rightful place."

"How is it you have come to me?" Quintero quizzed the men.

"We first spoke with a man named Steve Ivory. He gave us directions to you."

"Yes, I suppose he would," Quintero returned. "I have expected someone from your family for many years; yet the seasons passed one after another, until this day."

"Do you have the cross?" one inquired.

"Can anyone own something of such beauty? No, I have only its memory. For it, like a beautiful woman encountered in one's life, can only be drawn upon from time to time as a pleasant thought. To have it otherwise, would put one's life in a state of turmoil. For something of such beauty always catches another's eye."

"I see what you mean," one of the men returned, but not satisfied he inquired further, "Do you know what became of the cross?"

"Perhaps." found Quintero's lips, and escaped before he could clinch them tightly.

The look of excitement showed on the three Mexicans' face. Quintero noticing this waved his arms, as if to discount his statement.

"What is it that you would give to possess it?" Quintero inquired, then continuing he answered for them. "Hector Antonne gave his life. Before him the Sly One risked his, then finally your grandfather gave his health. What are you willing to give to have it?"

The three men, with squared shoulders, stood silently before Quintero. He could see the determined look he once saw in Señor Antonne's eyes in theirs. He turned and started to walk towards his home.

"Señor Ivory asked us to tell you that Miss Wink has returned to her father's ranch."

Quintero froze in mid step, turning and facing the three men. His heart leapt with excitement as he anticipated the thought of seeing her once more. "This was good medicine," he reasoned.

His mind wandered for a moment, to a place far away. He envisioned a scene that had portrayed itself over and over in his mind. Pausing for a moment he turned and walked closer to the three men.

"There is now, as we speak, an old man, a war chief, named Goyathlay, to many he is called Geronimo. The last great war chief of my people who waits like all to pass into the void beyond. Yet he sits each day, longing to return to his former land, the land of his birth, a land he was uprooted from and taken far away as a prisoner. I have seen him in my dreams as sleep denied me. I have heard his voice call to me bidding me to come. His bones tire of carrying his weight; his eyes long to see the sun set one last time on the Dragoons.

"Where is this old chief that we might aid in his rescue?" one of the Mexicans inquired.

"In a place called Oklahoma," Quintero returned.

"I have been to Oklahoma," one of the men spoke. "It is very far from here. How is it we will be able to do this thing?" he finished.

Quintero scratched at the earth with his foot, then spoke, "I do not know of its entirety yet, but I have an idea."

"If we agree to help you, in return you will lead us to the golden cross?" The three men's eyes searched Quintero for his answer.

"Yes, it will be so," Quintero answered.

THE RESCUE
Chapter 21

"Quintero was a study in opposites, a throw back from the past, almost a savage, yet a gentleman if I ever saw one."

"What do you mean, Father?"

"Listen carefully and I will do my best to try to explain how all of this came to be:"

Raised with a craw full of learning from his people. He knew a lot of things needed fix'n. The blend of old and new needed stir'n a little. He was taught to hate the Mexicans. They tried to destroy his people; the Whites only finished the job. Yet he worked around those hatreds and befriended Hector Antonne and accepted him into the rank of brotherhood. He never quite got over the loss of this brother either. He mourned him until his death.

Quintero squeezed through a lock and kept the remnants of the old ways ongoing far longer than they would have without him. He should have been on the train to Florida with Geronimo, yet he remained behind to carry on the tradition that otherwise could have been lost.

The Grandson, like his Grandfather, followed the old ways. That is why the woman warrior Wink held him with such high regard. She, like him, was a bubble adrift in a windstorm, lost to what breeze would blow, yet, remaining a seed to possibly grow the future of a whole race. How can I judge them differently?

The three Mexicans warned me what Quintero had on his mind as they returned to Mexico. They were determined young men; I could see that. But even I did not comprehend how Quintero could be so bold as to dream the dream he had in mind, for it was near impossible.

Geronimo fought many battles, and was punished for them. Yet, here was a Medicine Man who still followed the old ways, and dared dream big enough to include the old Chief.

I waited for spring to return; it not only brought the new grass but it cleared the mind of winter and sent it on its way. The mind to do nothing but watch the snow fill the windward side of the house. To watch it grow deep like years past, until no more are the visions of youth rehearsed as sleep finds the unwary soul.

Quintero knew better than to tempt the hand of the Whites. He had worked a lifetime untouched by it. While others were imprisoned for their doings, he remained a shadow in a thicket moving around hidden by a place afforded him amongst the branches.

How is it that I became involved in this? It was simple enough. I could not refuse when asked by Quintero to escort Miss Wink, the woman warrior, to him. Unbeknown to me, I would be caught up in a storm that could break the earth in half. For it is known the Apache roots reach to the center of the earth, and what Quintero had in mind would test their strength. No longer would gold be enough to tempt one such as I, for ahead lie places and things able to parlay one's very soul into the unknown, testing the bindings placed by the Whites around the home of the red man, the Apache.

The three Mexicans were to return in the spring, when the snow quit coming to the deserts of Southeastern Arizona. Miss Wink and I had visited many times as winter knocked at our door, and we knew this day would come, for it had been laid from the beginning. Spring followed the days mentioned. It was not my doing, but the doing of the Great Ones who framed this earth. I only had to wait in anticipation, knowing this day would arrive.

I drove my automobile out to the Irishman's ranch; he greeted me in the front yard. He no longer harbored resentment towards the unknown, for he knew Wink was a child of the mountains, these deserts, and him lastly. He piled her belongings into the back seat of my automobile and we headed back towards Willcox. He watched as we turned the bend, leaving the rocks behind that marked the road to town. Wink waved until her father passed into the distance.

The horse, like the Apache, had seen the sun set on its era. No longer would it, or he, come sweeping down upon the unwary, for its time had also drawn nigh. Now it grazed outside the home of the red man, waiting to be called once more for duty; yet it was not meant to be. Time had changed somewhere in the middle of somewhere, changing that what which familiar into something unknown. That is why, as the automobile backfired, while turning the last corner heading into town, I clinched my teeth and tightened my grasp upon the wheel. For I knew the horse would never again hold the place he once did. My determination remained unwavering. I would tame this four-wheeled beast; the rough roads would only slow change down somewhat. Fate had reasoned it so.

Mary did not understand what I was about to do, nor could she reason how I came to find all the gold I possessed. Yet she seemed to understand as I drove up with Miss Wink and parked in front of our house that there was something more than I was able to explain. Like the Irishman before mentioned she knew something was there that was not to be shared.

The grade was steep as we pulled up the mountain heading towards Steins, New Mexico. Lordsburg waited beyond and there the broad plains would allow easier travel to Pinos Altos. The Apache knew this land better than I, for it was their home. The peaks of the Gilas, still covered in snow, invited me onward. There, the mountain spirits resided, high above the desert we traveled. Yet I, like any stranger in time, sailed into this land on a craft of steel, that belched fire and turned on wheels of rubber, barely able to hold its own against a land of rock and forest slope.

Quintero and the three Mexicans were waiting at Piños Altos. Their horses were parlayed with some Hot Springs Apaches. Quintero arranged for their care until our return.

I've seen a comet streak across the sky, leaving a trail from horizon to horizon. The scale of which is unparalleled by other forces found in nature. The energy there of is real and vibrant. There is one however that comes close, it is love. A power that leads one to think more of another than ones self. I offer this example of the feeling in the air when Quintero and the woman warrior Wink met again at Piños Altos. The energy between the two could be felt. It had power; it moved things in its wake. I knew it was going to be different this time. Wink had not found happiness on her return to Ireland. Her greatest fear had become real; she, being with child, could not convince her husband she had been attacked by three men and forced to endure their unwanted advances. He, feeling betrayed, ended their marriage. She, using all the determination that a mother possessed, brought her two sons, back to her desert home. She was now free to pursue happiness in what form it found her.

Quintero had spent a long winter sorting out his thoughts about the coming spring. He had plenty of time to do so. Rehearsing things in his mind helped him deal with his loneliness. His wife, once more heavy with child, had decided to return to her people in Acoma, New Mexico. It was within her right to do so. The Apache allowed this custom and it extended for several years. This gave the mother and child both time to grow under the watchful eyes of the woman's family. She had not returned to her village since her youth. Quintero did not begrudge her for going. The silence, however, was deafening and the loneliness without his children bit at him. This same reasoning gave him the right to take another wife in her absence; it was the Apache way.

He knew love, yet he submitted to its power and became a part of the fire and ice that it brings. Once he had resisted its power. Now in the arms of Wink once more, the force that binds man and woman settled upon the two.

Countless miles lay ahead and behind of this mismatched journey. The land of the Apache passed into the beyond as we struggled over hill and plains. Grasslands, devoid of buffalo, stretched on every horizon. The ribbons of steel winding across this sea of grass became our compass. Occasionally, a locomotive pulling several cars passed by us. A scream from the locomotive, as it belched steam from its whistle, always accompanied its passing. Acknowledgements from the passengers made it complete. Each going they're separate way, marveling at the other and wondering silently as to where the other was heading. The stars at night were the only things we recognized. Yet, our spirits remained high at the prospects of succeeding at what we endeavored.

The Mexicans brought clothes for Quintero from Mexico. They trimmed his hair so he resembled one of them, at least enough to fool the average person. The tin lizzie became a rolling magazine. Rifles and handguns plus ammunition were stored in the rear, easily accessible. Yet the days passed peacefully, as if miles alone were enough to keep an attempt of this kind from happening.

At night, around the campfire, Quintero would don his buckskin and once more be himself. The songs of old filled the air as he greeted the rise and fall of the sun. He and the woman would steal away at times and their laughing and splashing in the water could be heard in camp. It was those times I missed Mary and the boys the most. Yet, I also missed the youth of another time. I, too, held a song in my heart and lamented the change.

I would like to say we reached our destination without calling attention to ourselves. This was not so, however, as everyone, it seemed for miles, gathered as we passed each dwelling and fell in behind us. By the time we reached the Indian Agency, we had a large crowd assembled. However, it was not us they focussed their interest on, but the automobile. Covered in dust, it was not placed in its best light; yet it still held the crowd's attention.

Wink, in her perfect Irish accent, told the crowd we were from a Wild West show, and were there to pay Geronimo a visit. Much to our astonishment, we learned that the Old Warrior was absent and had been taken to another town two days before.

"What do we do now?" I asked.

Looking at the ground, Quintero responded, "We wait."

We backtracked to a river bottom we had passed. There we made camp. Many of the Indians followed us. They held their distance and allowed us to make camp under their watchful eye. They seemed perfectly harmless. Once more their attention was upon the automobile. One by one they left us and returned to their homes as darkness approached. A particularly curious young man drew closer than the others. Wink approached him and asked him if he understood the white man's words?

"Yes," he replied.

Wink then told him to tell Geronimo, when he returned, that we wished to talk with him.

The young man followed the others, and once again we were by ourselves.

The days passed slowly as we waited for the return of Geronimo. On the third morning I awoke and took a walk down by the stream we camped by. An old Indian man sat on the bank fishing. A large tree grew nearby, offering shade. I walked closer and watched him fish. It was not long until he spoke to me. The words were cautious at first, then, in time, spoken more freely.

"What brings you here?" he asked.

"We seek audience with Geronimo," I returned.

"Which Geronimo do you seek?" He spoke softly as he fussed with the willow pole he fished with.

"Is there more than one?" I answered.

"There is only one Goyathlay. (Geronimo) Yet many come to glance at a man who is no more."

"What do you mean?" I asked.

"Geronimo is only a man, some would make more of him than what there is," he said as he again focused on fishing.

"Has Geronimo returned yet?"

"Yes, he is here now," the old man said.

"Does he know we are waiting for him?"

"Yes," the old man said.

"When will he come to see us?" I asked.

"I am here now," the old man assured me.

"You are Geronimo, then?" I quizzed the old man.

"Yes," he once more answered me, with a grin on his face.

I couldn't believe I was face to face with the old War-horse and didn't even know it. I excused myself for a moment, and walked the short distance to our camp.

"Quintero!" I said. "Geronimo waits down by the creek. He is fishing at the swimming hole."

Quintero and Wink headed towards Geronimo. The three Antonnes' and I followed close behind.

Quintero did not say anything to Geronimo. Instead, he walked close to him and sat down silently. He waited for Geronimo to speak. Geronimo did not focus his eyes upon Quintero, but instead fussed with his fishing line. We watched from a short distance. Finally, Geronimo broke the silence:

"I am here as you asked. What is it that you have come for?"

"I am Quintero, keeper of the secret places of our homeland."

Geronimo studied the younger man for a moment, as if in disbelief of what his ears had just heard.

"How have you found me?" Geronimo asked, staring at Quintero.

"With the help of these, my friends," Quintero returned.

He extended his arm in our direction, giving visual affirmation he meant us.

"I have come to return you to our homeland, so you can resume your place as Chief over our people."

Geronimo looked sad as Quintero spoke. He was in deep thought, searching for the right words to respond to Quintero.

"Many years have I been away from my home. It does my heart good to know that there are those who would welcome me back. It is true that I am still War Chief over my people. But my people are spread to many places and I am but one. I am at peace and will soon die here in this foreign place, as the great father in Washington looks the other way. My years are now many, and time moves faster now than in my youth."

"That is why we have come to this place, to return you to your former home with us," Quintero finished.

"And how can this be?" Geronimo asked.

"We have guns and ammunition, weapons of all kinds. We stand as warriors, waiting for your command," Quintero offered.

"I should go to battle with my former enemies by my side?" Geronimo rebuked. "And would they battle against, the soldiers of their kind?

They would fight to the death at your side," assured Quinero.
Geronimo cast a stern glance at our direction. "No, my place is here. I will bring no more sorrow upon my people. If I went, where would I go? They would search everywhere for me. It would be as before."

"They would not find you," Quintero assured him

"And where could I escape the fury of the Longknives? Geronimo inquired.

"There is one place," Quintero returned. Sno-ta-hay."

"Sno-ta-hay," Geronimo said, pondering the word. Yes, that could be possible," he reasoned. Silence prevailed, and then he continued thoughtfully, "Still, I will stay here. Let's speak no more on this matter."

The rest of the day was spent in conversation. Geronimo had not heard news of his former home for so long that he kept Quintero busy for hours, filling in some of the blank spots in his knowledge of his former life. They spoke English and Apache, often bouncing back and forth; I listened for awhile, guessing what they were saying to each other. In time, I grew tired of trying to second-guess the two men.

I must admit, my major interest in life was searching for gold. That is why I stood up and excused myself and headed back to camp. "Sno-ta-hay," I said to myself out loud. "Where have I heard this before?" I walked over to a shade tree and sat down, leaning against its large trunk. Deep in thought, my mind wandered to a time many years earlier, as I camped in a similar spot by the San Francisco River, in Arizona Territory. The evening grew long as I cooked beans upon a bed of mesquite coals. I heard horses approaching. I stood up, trying to get a fix on who was riding into my camp. Several horsemen soon stood around the fire. They introduced themselves to me one by one. Adams, the only one I remember now years later, said he and his fellows were searching for a fabulous gold mine in a canyon named Sno-ta-hay. I'd never heard this name again until that day as Quintero spoke to Geronimo. It all began to fit in my mind, The Lost Adams' Digs, The Lucky Boy Mine, The Mine on Grasshopper Ridge and Sno-ta-hay, they all have to be one and the same!

That evening, Geronimo returned to our camp, carrying his lance. A long strand of beads hung from his neck. He was still an impressive sight, even in his old age. Once more Quintero and he spoke. This time a large fire burned in the clearing we were camped in.

Quintero spoke first, "We will go tomorrow, my Chief."

"That is good," Geronimo returned.

"Will you reconsider?" Quintero asked.

"No, that would not be wise," Geronimo spoke. "I would that you go as you came. One thing, however, should change, I see that love has looked upon you." He summoned the woman Wink. "I desire that you become a wife to care for this great man." With that he put her hand into Quintero's. He then took Quintero's free hand and put it into Wink's. "I would that you be a husband and care for this woman. Now, I desire you to live the old way, the way it was when we were a people. Go to our former homeland in Mexico, the land of these three men," he said, as he pointed to the Antonnes. "Find the deepest parts of the Sierra Madre, and there make a home and have children. Teach them the old way that it will not die."

Geronimo told Quintero to give the Cross of St. Stephen to the three Mexicans. He said it was rightfully theirs. Quintero was thereby relieved of the oath he made to his grandfather. This took a lot of weight from his mind.

The following morning we headed for home. The automobile roared to life, and we bounced over rock and plains until Piños Altos came into view. There I parted with Quintero and Wink. We agreed to meet in a month at Stockton Pass, where he would deliver the cross.

I took the three Antonne brothers to Dos Cabezas and showed them the place Hector had been killed. I also shared with them how the golden cross was found by a bear, and unearthed by it. Otherwise, it might still be lost to this day. They did not appear to understand the significance of this, nor did I until I got to know Quintero and the Apache way.

The month passed, and we rode for Stockton Pass.

"Love looks well on my two friends," I said, as we rode into Quintero and Winks' camp; smiles on their faces were their reply.

"Is the cross here?" one of the Mexicans inquired.

Quintero walked over to his belongings and pulled out a buckskin bag. He removed it, allowing the sun to once more dance upon the beautiful object.

The three men fell upon their knees. Quintero handed it to the closest man. Hands trembling, he gently passed it to the next, the cross finally coming to rest in the third man's hands.

"Magnificent!" one of the men said as he kissed the cross' surface.

"It is done," Quintero said to me as we watched the three men study the cross. "If it is not meant for the cross to leave Apache soil, then the Mountain Spirits will once more see to it that it is lost. It is no longer my concern."

Returning to Wink's side; they fussed over some of their possessions.

It was early enough that I could put miles between this place and myself, so I tried to say my farewells, Quintero would not have any of that.

"Stay with us," he said as he encouraged me to have a seat by him. "I want you to meet my son," Quintero said proudly.

It was not long until a young man came dragging in some firewood. You could not help notice the striking resemblance between Quintero and his son. The same mannerisms, the same proud way he walked, left no room for doubt that the same blood flowed in this youngsters veins; Apache blood.

"How did you find things at your home?" I asked, trying to make small talk.

"Things were not well," Quintero returned.

"What do you mean?" I encouraged him.

"The mother of my children, my first love, has gone on ahead to the land of the Spirits. She died giving birth while I was away."

What do you say to a person who has suffered such a loss? I was without words that could express my sympathy, so I remained quiet out of respect. Quintero could see how I felt; he tried to show me that he understood.

"Will you ride with us a short while?" he asked me.

"Where will we go?" I said.

"I want you to see a special place called Metate Mound. It's not far from here."

The Mexicans took their leave the following morning. I rode with the Indians to Metate Mound. I could see outlines of stone buildings that once stood upon this place sticking from the earth. Evidence was scattered everywhere indicating the Redman's former occupations. At the edge of a small clearing was a freshly made cedar wiki-up; inside were stored belongings of my friends. I walked closer, wanting to examine its method of construction.

"What is this?" I asked Quintero as I pointed to a small curious object hanging in the doorway.

"It is a child's sandal. It belonged to one who passed this way many journeys ago."

"Oh," I said as I examined its workmanship. "Very nicely woven," I acknowledged.

That night we sat around a small campfire. I asked Quintero what he would do now that so much had changed in his life.

"I will do as my Chief said," he replied. "I will go to the Sierra Madres and see if a place exists where the Apache can live as before."

We scattered the beads from Geronimo's necklace upon Metate Mound. Next, we buried the lance he gave us, as he asked us to do. They await the return of his spirit to this, his homeland. Quintero sang a song, as he did so well, and it was over.

The years passed and many times I visited with Wink as she returned home to visit her father. She spoke of their many children and of the place where they found refuge. Others joined them there as they lived out their dreams.

"Father, what about the stone bear?"

"Miss Wink placed it around my neck as I prepared to ride from Metate Mound. I've worn it every since."

Steve Ivory fussed with the leather cord around his neck as he often did. Twisting it one way, then another. The stone bear attached to it, worn smooth by the years, no longer carried the eagle feather it once did. The years had taken its toll.

After pausing for a long breath; and looking off into the distance, as if he was surveying a moment of his past. Smiling, he softly said, "The gold is out there you know, it's out there.

Now when the old men gather, they speak in hushed voices of Quintero. Some think he was a legend. Others say they knew him and last saw him down by the Stronghold. One speaks up and silences the rest.

"Quintero's out there someplace, you know. He is always watching and wandering around. I saw him while rounding up cattle last fall. The power is in him, and he guards the secret places. As I spoke to him, I could see flakes of gold shining in his hair. Now you tell me what this means? I did not ask him how they got there. I just hurried on my way. I was afraid."

A purple peak afar,
A red monument to the south,
Can you see him?
There he sits; legs crossed.
Over there in the shadows,
Quintero, or his grandson,
The keepers, the ones who know,
When the sun strips the shadows
He is gone, or is he?

YELLOW METAL

CRY OF THE EAGLE

THE QUINTERO
SAGA CONTINUES

by
Paul W. LeBaron

Available summer of 2002

1

THE CRYING BABY
CHAPTER I

The Indian, barely a child herself, was in the final stages of labor. Soon the baby would come. She bit soundly on a piece of leather. This kept her jaw muscles tensed, unable to let any sound escape her lips. The sound kept inside wished to declare to the world it is done. She bent forward and caught the child as it emerged into the world.

A light snow fell steadily; soon the ground would be covered in white. The new mother quickly wrapped the baby in a blanket and tended to her own needs as best she could. She felt an urgency to return to her people. Beads of sweat ran down her cheeks as she hurried onward. A quick motion of her hand and her robe was over her head. The snow stung her face as it hurled itself against her. She headed towards the sound of the barking dogs at the village. Her mother's warm fire awaited her. She drew back the blanket hanging over the doorway, went inside and collapsed on the floor. The baby's crying filled the room.

In the corner, the girl's parents squatted by a fire roasting pieces of meat. The woman stood up and walked over to examine her grandchild. She bent over, picked up the baby and carried it over and placed it in front of the man. He smiled at the baby and bent forward placing his head against it. A feather was sticking out of a crack in a timber supporting the roof. He reached up, retrieved the feather and lovingly tickled the baby on the face. Soaking in the warmth of the fire, the newborns' facial expressions changed as the feather tickled it.

The woman's attention returned to the new mother; the delivery went well. Relieved she cradled her daughter's head in her lap. She ran her fingers around a curl of the girl's hair. It was not long, she thought, since the day her daughter, whom she now held in her arms, was born. A night much like this one brought her. Wolves cried out in hunger in the distance. The river bottom willows offered little protection if they should decide to attack. The cold and snow seemed to always be there on such a night, yet she endured. Now, here she was holding the same baby in her arms. This time, though, it was her daughter who endured the continuation of life.

The baby's persistent crying woke the new mother. She had not been asleep long, she stood up and walked over by the fire and picked up the baby. She put it to her breast and let it nurse her. The baby, now content, resumed sleeping. Milk flowed freely from both breasts and ran down her stomach. She found some soft material and let it absorb the milk. The new mother, like the child, was soon sleeping. Her dreams carried her back to a summers day, a short time ago, visitors from a village of her father's people had come to celebrate with them. One was taller and stronger than the others. She caught him looking at her. She blushed and turned her head quickly. His stares continued to follow her as she worked with her mother preparing food in front of their house. Later, he brought some rabbits he had hunted and put them at her doorway. He left without revealing himself; still she knew they were from him.

One day, while filling an olla of water at a spring near the village, he stepped out of some shrubs growing along the trail. The startled girl almost dropped the water jug. He grabbed it to prevent it from falling. She reached out for the olla of water. He grabbed her hand and tried to hold it, but she pulled back and demanded the water; he refused and held tightly to the water jug. The girl turned and walked towards the village empty handed. The young man followed along behind her carrying the water, all the while chiding her trying to regain her attention. On the edge of the clearing he paused and told her he would go no further. This suited her as well since she wanted no one to see her with him. She took the olla of water and walked quickly towards home.

The following evening, the young man was once again waiting for her as she returned to the spring. It was no surprise to her this time. She figured she hadn't seen the last of him. He approached her and asked if he might carry the water for her. She smiled at him and handed him the heavy jug of water; she had filled it extra full. The young man carried it without complaint. Upon reaching the edge of the tree line, the young girl took the olla from him and dumped some of the water on the ground before she would carry it onward. The man gave her a scornful look knowing he had been outsmarted.

The girl did not return for water the next day. The young man waited in his usual place, but to no avail. So he began to find excuses for hanging around her part of the village. He spotted her, the following morning, as her mother and her went out to forage for food. He waited until they had split up and out of sight of each other before he crept close to her. He threw a small pebble to attract her attention. The girl looked at him and motioned for him to go away. The young man shook his head, and motioned for her to come closer. She did, and on this day love found it's way inside her and there grew into the child now born to her.

Morning appeared suddenly to the desert; the sun did battle with the darkness holding the village in its grip. Daylight won. Soon warmth began melting the light snow that had fallen the night before. The man was the first to throw back the flap covering the entrance to their home. He walked swiftly to the kiva where the other men of the village had gathered. From the far side of the room a man stated, matter of factly, that he heard a baby crying in the night from his house. "Are you a new father?" He asked. The men in the room knew this was not so, yet the question needed to be asked. "My youngest daughter gave birth last evening." He replied. "How is this so? Since she has no man." The voice from the group returned. "Last spring, as I slept, one warm night I heard the sound of a flute. The sweetest sound I have ever heard. The sound became louder and clearer as it approached my home. I supposed it was coming from a neighbor. I enjoyed it and drifted off to sleep. Little did I know, it was the seducer Kokopelli tantalizing my ears with his music. It was this night he entered my daughter while she slept and made her with child. How else could this be since she has no man?" The group remained silent. The rover Kokopelli had been to the village before. He had seduced women in the past and fooled them with his magic. By no further discussion of the matter, they thereby agreed it must be so. The man rose to his feet and returned to his home.

The baby cried loudly, as the man entered the room. As his eyes became accustomed to the light, he could see the baby was alone. He went to the child and raised it up to him and bounced it lovingly. As he walked out side,. he drew the baby's wraps tightly around it. A lady who was working close by walked towards him and removed the baby from his arms and made a fuss over it. The man surveyed the surroundings trying to discover where his wife and daughter were. It worried him that the baby was alone. "Could this mean trouble was at hand?" He asked himself.

He returned to his house with the child and waited, hopping it was well with the women. The baby cried out in hunger, but the man could do little to comfort it.

The day was long; darkness once again would soon claim its rite to the hours of rest. He went outside and watched the sun retreat. In the distance he saw someone coming. As the person drew closer he could see it was his wife. He was happy to see her, but anguish burned in his stomach, for where was the child's mother?

The woman's face hung long, her eyes cast down. "What is wrong?" The man inquired of her. She continued to watch the ground as she told of how the girl had left early in the morning while he was in the kiva. I followed after her, trying to reason with her, as long as I could. I left only when I knew I had just enough time to reach home before nightfall.

The man handed the woman the baby. He hurried inside and put on his warmest clothes. His weapons were in the corner; he reached for them as he headed back to the doorway. He held the woman for a moment, and then he headed off into the darkness.

He camped for what was left of the night where the two women were together last. He could still see the girl's tracks but was to tired to go on. The cold embraced him as he lay on the ground. A cedar tree offered him what it could, but as the wind picked up the cold stung at him with its fury.

He longed for the warmth of his home. He had worked hard to obtain what comforts he had. His dwelling consisted of three rooms; a storage room contained food they had grown, corrugated ollas held maize, enough to eat until the next harvest was ready. Dried pumpkins and melons also were stored there. Racks of meat hung in the darkest corner drying. A metate, that had been handed down from ancestors, took the honored position in the middle of the room. A large olla was buried in the earth at one end. A quick motion of the hand and the meal would be swept into this olla until needed. The second room adjoined the storage room. The cooking was done here. Also food was stored around the perimeter of the room. In one corner, weavings at different stages of completion were piled. Tobacco leaves hung from the ceiling, in the opposite corner. The final room was where they slept. During the day mats were rolled back and this room was also used for living.

He had lived at this village for many seasons. He labored hard during his stay with his wives people. When he was not farming or hunting for food, he made long strands of beads. Black jet and brown soapstone were his staples. Occasionally a passerby from another village would trade him turquoise. This stone was his favorite. His trade was in demand, and he grew wealthy.

The village rested on a small bench above a river draining a vast forest. Stone cliffs formed a natural barrier between the desert he called home and the forest. He was born to a people who lived beyond the cliff and forest on a vast red desert in the high country. It was many days journey, he had not returned for several seasons. His father and mother had returned to the world of Spirits. So he had grown content with his wife's people.

Now, all of this had changed. Necessity had made him leave all of this behind and search for his daughter, a part of him that still brought him joy. Why had she not entrusted him with her secret plans? He rose to his feet, shook off the cold and continued the search. The wind picked up as daylight found him on the move. By mid morning all of the girl's tracks were gone; the wind had erased them. The man paused upon a high point in the trail; he looked long in all directions. He yelled as loud as he could, but to no avail. He rose to his feet again and continued; the red outline of the distant mountains beckoned him onward. Landmarks, he knew in his youth, pointed the way.

After many days he reached his former village. A brother still lived, he found out. He informed him of the urgency of his visit. "The girl seeks the father of her child."

"Why is it she would search for him here? None but yourself has taken a wife from the village you now live in. I feel that the flute-playing wayfarer is to blame. Why is it she would leave the child and search for one whom used his music to have his way with her? Was not the child enough to prove his cunning? How will she find one she has not seen? Is he not like a bird singing from a bush; one walks closer and finds the music is coming from the next and so on. Tonight we will meet with the men of this village; the Old One has summoned us. We will inquire there if any know of the whereabouts of your daughter.

The village elders filed out, one after the other until the Kiva was silent. One man, now sleeping, remained. Unaware that the others had left, head slumped forward, was oblivious to his surroundings. Sacred stones spilled down his lap onto the Kiva floor. His hand still clinched the one which moments before allowed him a glimpse of the future. It was this that drained the Old One of his strength. Barely able to convey to the others what he had seen before it failed, he now rested.

This message was different then the others, usually the Old One answered the needs of the people in the village. Proclaiming the time to plant and harvest. Summoned moisture in dry times and predicted the changing of climate. This time however, the men looked at each other across the fire circle, watching for any sign of unbelief in the words the old man spoke. Words of change, words of uncertainty in a land unchanging for the many seasons of bygone times.

No words were spoken as the men climbed the ladder, leaving the smoke filled entrance behind. The chill of the wind, hurrying across the broad grasslands, tugged at their wraps, as they struggled on their way. A few flakes of snow stung their faces, as it was given extra velocity by the wind. The barking dogs greeted them, as they drew closer to their destination. Warmth waited inside, yet the words of the Old One spread a chill that could not be warmed by fire.

The following night they came once more to the Kiva. In-groups of two or three, they silently climbed down the ladder into the bowels of the earth from whence they came. Each sat cross-legged around the fire, all eyes focusing upon the Ancient One in the corner of the room. Unsure of how long it would be until he spoke they had waited long into the night before they entered the Kiva, now they were all there, from the most respected to the least. All ears were at the Old Ones disposal to do with as he pleased.

The two brothers sat in a place of prominence. The recent return of one of their own allowed them that. Now, as silence continued, their eyes surveyed those around them. Many faces from their youth brought remembrances of former pleasant times, most noticeable, was the patience in which all waited to hear the words of the Old One.

A cough preceded movement by the Old One. Finally his head raised, he looked around the room, acting surprised, so many faces staring at him.

"I have seen now the reason of my great concern," he began. "Many times have I tried to find what causes the uneasiness in my mind. Now I know of certainty, that men come who will change our lives, in so much as to destroy us if we let them. I've seen them astride beasts, larger than buffalo, akin to the stature of the mighty elk. They clothe themselves in coverings sufficient to with stand the blow of club or arrow. They now approach us from the south. For many lifetimes peace held us in its arms, acting as a loving mother to us. Differences were put aside as brother lived with brother for the common good of all. I see now a new day is born when this will surely change." His voice grew weak and tapered off to reach inaudible tones, then once more silence returned.

The men filed out as they came without making a sound. They left the Kiva and returned to the village.

The following day came casting uncertainty over the village in light of the recent words of the Old One. All tongues were busy interpreting what they meant.

These were simple farmers who scratched out a living in the red clay, high desert country. A land of wind, a land of stark beauty shaped by the millennium into a place of opposites. A place of life, and a place of death. Each waiting its turn to play a man. To shape him just as it shaped the land itself.

Precious little fat hung on the land. The old clung to whatever knowledge enabled them to be of the most worth, thereby increasing their chance of survival to a ripe old age. In a land of unwritten past a good memory brought much prestige.

The winds picked up in the night and the temperature plummeted. The village dogs wedged themselves into the deepest recesses where warmth could be assured.

The seasons, like roots of a mighty tree, anchor one to his beginnings. As one day passes, a new one is forming. A breath first enters, then leaves a man. Can one measure the good accomplished? Only in the end can one asses whether it be good or bad.

The earth yielded its abundance, when blessed with the proper amount of moisture. It is therefore an act of all things common that enables a man to reap the harvest of good years. Misfortune is not numbered among those of little means, for it extols nothing of value. Therefore it is but a waste of remembrance, the oldest among the village waste no time in endearing sorrow to those whom would listen. Abundant yields, whether it is crops or riches, assure a successful future. One day at a time, one good endeavor, gives all in common something solid to build upon.

The Old One spoke of change, of time soon when the earth would withdraw her nurturing hand and withhold her peace she had upheld them in for so long. It was change most feared by the people, yet the future would come as will. "All would see," the Old One declared.

The two brothers prepared ground cornmeal into mush and sat in comfort by a small fire eating their morning meal.

"I have journeyed many days to reach Hawikuh, my former home. My heart is full of joy seeing so many dear to me. On the other side of my being I sorrow for the loss of my child, a piece of me that brought so much beauty to my life."

"Yes, my brother, I feel your great sorrow and I want to extend to you all that I have, the comfort of my home, my food, all this is yours as well as my heart." He placed his hand over his chest to emphasize the words that he spoke. "I have made inquires and none come forward with knowledge of the missing girl."

"What of the words the Old One speaks, does truth flow from his mouth?"

"The Old One is our great uncle in our mother's family. Many times has he brought the rain to our crops when all others attempts failed. I put my belief in his words. Trading parties returning from the land southward bring seashells and brightly colored feathers from exotic birds along with all manner of trinkets. They also return with words, these words tell of men much like those described by the Old One. I believe in my heart they are on their way to us, since that is what he says."

"Then my heart also sorrows for my people, for our way of life seems threatened, perhaps by a force far greater than ours. I must take leave of this place and return to the search for my daughter. I shall enter each village along my travels and inquire of her. Words of warning delivered by the Old One shall I leave at each doorstep I cross."

The two men stood and squeezed each other's hand. One ducked under the doorway and was gone. Sorrow hung on both hearts, for good-byes were uncertain in these times.

The cotton wood trees, lining the riverbanks, looked like skeletons as he crossed the divide and looked down into the valley his village was in. Perhaps this was a premonition to what lay ahead, he worried.

The wind pushed against him as he entered his village. A baby's crying filled his ears, she has returned, he thought as he ran the final distance to his home. He climbed the ladder quickly and threw back the blanket sealing the entrance.

"The children?" the man asked. "I heard the baby crying," he said.

"Yes, I heard crying as well. Have you found her?" the woman searched beyond him. The emptiness answered this question for her.

"The baby?" the man countered.

"The baby now nurses on the breast of a relative and grows each day."

"What is it that fooled me?" the man said as he turned to face the fire.

"The earth mourns for the loss of our daughter. At first light the wind blows from the valley. It sounds as a mother crying for her child. At night it returns from the mountains and sounds as a baby crying for its mother."

The man reached for the woman and held her close.

"Yes, that must be it," he said.

The woman began to weep. The man held her tighter.

"Strange, he said to her, I have never noticed it before."

In time the wind alone spoke these things of former glory. Now the unknowing walks, unaware that beneath the mound of earth once greatness stood. It is from this, words call out. Yet can one find words? Once spoken they are but wind building a sand dune or pushing against a monument thought to be unmovable, but in time reduced to naught. Hidden in the silence is words if one would hear.

ABOUT THE AUTHOR:

A second grade teacher introduced the author to the American Indian. She shared her love for them with each member of her class. The seed grew into a life long interest that still holds him captivated. That interest soon interwove with the history and lore of the Southwest, thereby becoming a love for both Indian and western tradition.

Arizona is home to numerous Indian tribes that trace their roots deep into native soil. Their heritage and traditions surround us.

One can not walk in Eastern Arizona with out virtually walking on history. Pieces of pre-historic pottery sherds dot the land, along with chips of stone, attesting to prior occupations. Ruins stand silently now, sentinels in lonely places. Once full of life and noise, now monuments to the past.

People lived and died in these silent places. The author attempts to place these people in real life situations, thereby, allowing a glimpse into their former lives.

Lonely canyons echo, as the coyote gives warning. It sends chills up ones spine. The shadows lend a mystery behind every tree and boulder. From them, a thousand pair of eyes, watching from the distance, waiting across the bridge of time. This is their land, the coyote, their voice.

At times, the author makes a humble attempt to do the same.

The author lives with his wife and family in the heart of the west at Snowflake, Arizona, surrounded by a melting pot of cultures and traditions, each ripe with mystery and intrigue.